Bookkeeping and Double-Entry Bookkeeping

Rose Mary Lynch

Gill & Macmillan

Gill & Macmillan Ltd

Goldenbridge

Dublin 8

with associated companies throughout the world

© Rose Mary Lynch 1996

0 7171 2408 8

Print origination in Ireland by DTP Workshop

Contents

Part 1 Bookkeeping Principles

Part 2 Bank Reconciliation

Part 3 Review

Abbreviations

a/c	account
b/d	brought down
cb	cash book
c/d	closing down
Cheq. no.	cheque number
cl	creditors ledger
CN no.	credit note number
cr	credit on bank statement
Cr	credit column in ledger
CRS	creditors
C/T	credit transfer
D.D.	direct debit
dl	debtors ledger
dr	debit on bank statement
Dr	debit column in ledger
DRS	debtors
F	folio
gj	general journal
gl	general ledger
Inv. no.	invoice number
pcb	petty cash book
pdb	purchases day book
prdb	purchases returns day book
R/D	refer to drawer
sdb	sales day book
srdb	sales returns day book

Introduction

This book is intended to cover the course for the Bookkeeping and Double-Entry Bookkeeping examinations at National Council for Vocational Awards Level 2.

Part 1 is designed to provide students with a thorough knowledge of basic bookkeeping principles. It is set out in chapters with short explanations and worked examples. Each chapter will have examples that will build on the content of the previous chapters. There follows at the end of each chapter a series of questions testing the subject content taught. Much of the emphasis in the last chapter of this section will be on exam-style questions, many examples of which are supplied. Emphasis will be placed on explaining the bookkeeping terms that arise throughout each chapter, as a way of preparing the students for Section C of the exam paper.

Part 2 introduces the students to bank reconciliation, including reasons for preparing a bank reconciliation statement. A worked example is given, taking the students through the various steps involved with a strong emphasis placed on explaining why. This is to give the students experience and understanding so that they can deal with errors that will arise (in both the cash book and on the bank statement). Emphasis will be placed on questions where the students have to compare the cash book and bank statement to find the entries to record in the updated bank account and the bank reconciliation statement.

Part 3 gives the students an opportunity to revise theory based on the bookkeeping covered in previous sections.

Chapter 1

Opening General Journal

The general journal (gj) is used to record unusual entries. There are several types of general journals. We will first consider the opening general journal.

Definitions

The **OPENING GENERAL JOURNAL** is a list of a business's assets, liabilities and capital at the beginning of the month. These are the closing figures from the previous month, e.g. the closing figures for January are the opening figures for February.

An **ASSET** is something that a business owns, for example premises, cash, stock or money due from customers (debtors).

Opening asset balances are always shown in the debit column.

A **LIABILITY** is something that a business owes, for example a loan, bank overdraft or money owed to suppliers (creditors).

Opening liability balances are always shown in the credit column.

CAPITAL is the amount of money that is invested in the business. It will increase if the owner(s) leaves (leave) some of the profits in the business each year; it will decrease if business money or goods are taken by the owner for his/her own use. When this happens it is called 'drawings'. A business must account for all the money invested in it.

OPENING CAPITAL = OPENING ASSETS – OPENING LIABILITIES

POSTING is the recording in a ledger of the entries from the books of first entry, in this case the opening general journal to the ledgers.

There are three ledgers.

DEBTORS LEDGER (dl) is for keeping accounts of those who owe the business money, i.e. the business sold to them on credit.

CREDITORS LEDGER (cl) is for keeping accounts of those to whom the business owes money, i.e. the business purchased from them on credit.

GENERAL LEDGER (gl) is where all the other accounts are maintained, i.e. asset accounts, liability accounts, expense accounts, gains accounts, purchases, sales, purchase returns, sales returns and VAT accounts.

Each account is given a name. This refers to what has been recorded in it. In the traditional 'T' account approach, each account has two sides. The left-hand side is referred to as 'the debit side' and the right–hand is referred to as 'the credit side'. A continuous balance format may also be adopted. This is where debit, credit and balance columns are maintained rather than using two sides.

Rules for Posting

As the opening general journal is just a list of opening balances taken from the ledgers, we transfer them back to the ledgers to the same side. They are entered as balances brought down (b/d).

Debit column balances are recorded on the debit side.

Credit column balances are recorded on the credit side.

A column labelled 'F' is the folio column. Here we note where the double entry can be found. This allows for the tracing of a transaction through the books. The initials of the ledger and possibly an account number/page number are used.

Example

The following are the assets and liabilities of A. Bannon on January 1. Premises £50,000; Equipment £23,500; Cash £350; Bank £1,200; Debtors: B. Cooke £450, D. Evans £670; Bank loan £8,000; Capital ? Write up the opening general journal and post to the appropriate accounts.

Solution

Opening General Journal for January 1

	F	Debit(£)	Credit(£)
Assets			
Premises	gl	50,000	
Equipment	gl	23,500	
Cash	gl	350	
Bank	gl	1,200	
Debtors: B. Cooke	dl	450	
D. Evans	dl	670	
Liabilities			
Loan	gl		8,000
Capital	gl		68,170*
Being asset, liabilities and capital on this date.		£76,170	£76,170

* This had to be calculated as opening assets – opening liabilities = 76,170 – 8,000.

Posting

The following shows how the figures in the above example would be posted to the general ledger.

General Ledger

Premises a/c

		F	(£)			F	(£)
Jan 1	Balance b/d	gj	50,000				

Equipment a/c

		F	(£)			F	(£)
Jan 1	Balance b/d	gj	23,500				

Loan a/c

		F	(£)			F	(£)
				Jan 1	Balance b/d	gj	8,000

Capital a/c

		F	(£)			F	(£)
				Jan 1	Balance b/d	gj	68,170

Cash a/c

		F	(£)			F	(£)
Jan 1	Balance b/d	gj	350*				

Bank a/c

		F	(£)			F	(£)
Jan 1	Balance b/d	gj	1,200*				

Debtors Ledger

B. Cooke a/c

		F	(£)			F	(£)
Jan 1	Balance b/d	gj	450				

D.Evans a/c

		F	(£)			F	(£)
Jan 1	Balance b/d	gj	670				

* These would be recorded on the debit side of a cash book if a full question is being completed.

Alternative Ledger Presentation — Continous Layout

Date	Details	F	Debit (£)	Credit (£)	Balance* (£)
	General Ledger				
	Premises a/c				
Jan 1	Balance b/d	gj			50,000dr
	Equipment a/c				
Jan 1	Balance b/d	gj			23,500dr
	Loan a/c				
Jan 1	Balance a/c	gj			8,000cr
	Capital a/c				
Jan 1	Balance b/d	gj			68,170cr
	Cash a/c				
Jan 1	Balance b/d	gj			350dr
	Bank a/c				
Jan 1	Balance b/d	gj			1,200dr
	Debtors Ledger				
	B. Cooke a/c				
Jan 1	Balance b/d	gj			450dr
	D. Evans a/c				
Jan 1	Balance b/d	gj			670dr

* In this column 'dr' stands for debit and 'cr' for credit.

Short Questions

Complete each of the following.

1. _____ is the amount of money invested in a business.

2. Something a firm owns is called an _____.

3. _____ is owed back to the owner of a business.

4. When private expenses are paid with business money, it is called _____.

5. Calculate closing capital if opening capital is £65,000, profit £8,000 and drawings £1,250. _____

_____

_____

Questions

Write up the opening general journal for each of the following questions. Post to the relevant ledgers. Remember to fill in the folios.

Q1. Feb 1   Assets: Premises £45,000; Vehicles £24,000; Cash £248; Bank £650; Debtors: R. Smith £1,234, T. Wright £560.
Liabilities: Loan £5,600; Capital?

Q2. Mar 1   Assets: Land and buildings £56,000; Fixtures and fittings £14,000; Petty cash £100; Debtors: V. Ring £400, W. Snow £60.
Liabilities: Bank overdraft £900; Creditors: A. Brady £250; Capital?

Q3. Apr 1   Assets: Premises £55,000; Motor van £7,500; Cash £560; Debtors: F. Flynn £4,600, G. Grimes £800.
Liabilities: Bank overdraft £4,560; Loan £6,700; Capital?

Q4. May 1   Assets: Land and buildings £60,000; Computers £11,000; Cash £800; Bank £1,800; Debtors: I. Ryan Ltd £600, M. Hand £1,100.
Liabilities: Bank loan £13,000; Creditors: M. Reynolds £5,000, U. Phelan £620; Capital?

Chapter 2

Analysed Cash Book

All businesses need to record money received in and paid out. Money is paid either in cash or by cheque. Money is either lodged to the bank or kept in the till. There are two ways of recording these transactions: either in an analysed cash book with a debit and credit side or on a receipts page and payments page with the totals transferred to a ledger account to balance off.

All receipts are recorded on the debit side.

All payments are recorded on the credit side.

Transactions

Typical transactions made by a business would be:

1. **Expenses/overhead** payments of a business, e.g. rent and wages.
2. **Purchases** of goods refers to the items bought for resale. For example, the purchases of a supermarket would be food items for resale in the business.
3. **Purchase of assets for cash** is not 'purchases' as an asset is not goods for resale. For example, a cash register bought for £500 cash would be recorded by crediting the cash book with £500.

   Write 'equipment' in the details column and not 'purchases'.

   The equipment account in the general ledger not the purchases account would be debited with £500.
4. **Payments made to suppliers.**
5. **Receipts from customers.**
6. **Sales of goods** refers to the sale of stock by the business. This would be food and drinks by the supermarket. 'Stock' is another word for items for resale.
7. **Sale of an asset** is recorded separately to 'sales;. A motor van sold for £3,000 cash would be recorded by debiting the cash book with £3,000.

   'Motor van' and not 'sales' is recorded in the details column.

   The motor van account in the general ledger would be credited with £3,000.
8. **Drawings** refers to money taken by the business owner for his/her own use.

   Money taken is recorded on the credit side of the cash book and posted to the debit side of a drawings account in the general ledger.
9. **Contra entry** refers to a transaction recorded on both sides of the cash book. The double entry is between the cash column and the bank column. We denote a contra entry by a 'C' in the folio column. There is no posting of these entries to the ledger as the double entry has already been completed.

Example 1

If £200 cash was lodged to bank, how should this be posted?

Solution

Here we take the £200 out of cash by crediting the cash column with £200. We write 'bank' in details as this is where the double entry can be found. We debit the bank column with £200, i.e. lodging this amount. We write 'cash' in details thus showing where it is coming from.

Example 2

If £350 was withdrawn from bank for cash, how should this be posted?

Solution

To record this we credit the bank column with £350. We write 'cash' in details. We debit the cash column with £350 and we write 'bank' in details.

VAT

VAT stands for value added tax, which is a tax on goods and services. Some goods and services are not liable for VAT, e.g. food items and postage charges. Other goods are liable for VAT at 12.5%. The standard rate of VAT is 21%. VAT is regarded as an indirect tax, i.e. it is included in the price charged for goods. The business person collects this tax on behalf of the government. Monthly returns are made to the revenue commissioners. It is therefore very important for the business person to keep accurate VAT records. To record entries properly in the cash book, receipts and payments must be analysed so that a breakdown of total receipts and total expenses can be easily obtained under the various headings.

Money paid by cheque or money lodged is recorded in the bank column. Cash transactions are recorded in the cash column.

Example

Record the following in the cash book using analysis columns as indicated. Assume that all cheques received are lodged on the date received.

Receipts: Cash, Bank, Sales, VAT, Other

Payments: Cash, Bank, Purchases, VAT, Creditors, Other

May 1   Balance in cash £400, Bank overdraft £550.

May 2   Paid D. Smith £65 by Cheq. no. 2; Paid Wages £180 cash; Paid Advertising £120 Cheq. no. 3.

May 4   Cash purchases £80 + VAT @ 21%; Sales £660 + VAT @ 21% money lodged; E. Moore paid £700 by cheque.

May 6   Paid rent £320 by Cheq no 4; Paid C. Cooke £95 cash.

Solution

Analysed Cash Book

Debit															Credit
	Details	F	Cash (£)	Bank (£)	Sales excl VAT (£)	VAT 21% (£)	Drs (£)	Oth. (£)	Date	Details	F	Cheq. No.	Cash (£)	Bank (£)	Purch excl VAT (£)	VAT 21% (£)	Crs (£)	Oth. (£)
May 1	Balance		400						May 1	Balance			-	550				
May 4	Sales	gl		798.60	660	138.60			May 2	D. Smith	cl	2		65			65	
May 4	E. Moore	dl		700.00				700	May 2	Wages	gl		180					180
									May 2	Advert	gl	3		120				120
									May 4	Purch	gl		96.80		80	16.80		
									May 6	Rent	gl	4		320				320
									May 6	C. Cooke	cl		95.00				95	
									May 6	Balance c/d			28.20	443.60				
		£	400	1,498.60	660	138.60	700					£	400.00	1,498.60	80	16.80	160	620
May 6	Bal b/d		28.20	443.60														

Balancing Accounts

Any account with more than one entry in it needs to be balanced. This applies to the cash book, petty cash book and the ledger accounts. Balancing means that you account for the difference between the debit side and the credit side thus making the sides even, i.e. balancing off the account. The following is the procedure to use in balancing.

1. Add up both sides in your rough work. In the cash book from the previous example,

Dr cash total	=	400.00
Cr cash total	=	371.80
Balance	£	28.20

    Fill in the figures for the bank columns yourself

Dr bank total	=	
Cr bank total	=	_____
Balance	£	

2. Write in the balance on the side with the smallest total, usually done in red. This is called 'closing down the account' hence the c/d written after the word 'balance'.

3. Draw in the total lines at the same level on both sides. Fill in totals that are now the same.

4. Bring down the balance to the opposite side line underneath the total. The debit side in the answer above shows a balance b/d (brought down) of £28.20 cash and £443.60 bank.

The closing balances for one period are the opening balances for the next period.

Rules for Posting

In double-entry bookkeeping all transactions are recorded in two accounts. These reflect the two sides of the transaction. The cash book is part of the double entry as well as being a book of first entry. A book of first entry refers to the recording of information from source documents. In this case these are cheque stubs and receipts. If an expense is paid, then money decreases and the expense paid increases. We show this in the books by recording everything twice: once on the debit side of an account and once on the credit side of another account. The expense account is debited and the cash book is credited. The cash book shows the movement of money. In the ledgers we keep accounts for the corresponding transaction. The rule is very simple.

Debit in cash book –> Credit in ledgers

Credit in cash book –> Debit in ledgers

A useful rule is that the debit side (left side of cash book or ledgers) is used when the business gains. The credit side (right side of the cash book or ledgers) is used when the business loses.

The use of 'cb' in the folio column indicates that the entry was posted from the cash book.

Example continued
Solution

Debtors Ledger

E. Moore a/c

Date	Details	F	(£)	Date	Details	F	(£)
				May 4	Bank	cb	700.00

Creditors Ledger

D. Smith a/c

Date	Details	F	(£)	Date	Details	F	(£)
May 2	Bank	cb	65.00				

C. Cooke a/c

Date	Details	F	(£)	Date	Details	F	(£)
May 6	Cash	cb	95.00				

General Ledger

Sales a/c

Date	Details	F	(£)	Date	Details	F	(£)
				May 4	Bank	cb	660.00

VAT a/c*

Date	Details	F	(£)	Date	Details	F	(£)
May 4	Purch	cb	16.80	May 4	Sales	cb	138.60
May 6	Bal c/d		121.80				
			£138.60				£138.60
				May 6	Balance b/d		121.80

Wages a/c

Date	Details	F	(£)	Date	Details	F	(£)
May 2	Cash	cb	180.00				

Advertising a/c

Date	Details	F	(£)	Date	Details	F	(£)
May 2	Bank	cb	120.00				

Purchases a/c

Date	Details	F	(£)	Date	Details	F	(£)
May 4	Cash	cb	80.00				

Rent a/c

Date	Details	F	(£)	Date	Details	F	(£)
May 6	Bank	cb	320.00				

* Note that for purchases, sales, purchase returns and sales returns the VAT is recorded in a separate account.

Alternative Method for Recording Cash Received and Paid

Receipts page

Date	Details	F	Cash (£)	Bank (£)	Sales (£)	VAT (£)	Drs (£)	Other (£)
May 4	Sales	gl		798.60	660	138.60		
May 4	E. Moore	dl		700.00			700	
				1,498.60	660	138.60	700	

Payments page

Date	Details	F	Cheq. no.	Cash (£)	Bank (£)	Purch (£)	VAT (£)	Crs (£)	Other (£)
May 2	D. Smith	cl	2		65			65	
May 2	Wages	gl		180.00					180.00
May 2	Advert	gl	3		120				120
May 4	Purch	gl		96.80		80	16.80		
May 6	Rent	gl	4		320				320
May 6	C. Cooke	cl		95.00				95	
				371.80	505	80	16.80	160	620

General Ledger

Debit   **Credit**

Date	Details	F	(£)	Date	Details	F	(£)
May 1	Bal b/d		400.00	May 6	Payments	cb	371.80
	Receipts		—	May 6	Bal c/d		28.20
			400.00				400.00
May 6	Bal b/d		28.20				

Bank a/c

Date	Details	F	(£)	Date	Details	F	(£)
May 6	Receipts		1,498.60	May 1	Balance b/d		550.00
				May 6	Payments		505.00
				May 6	Bal c/d		443.60
			1,498.60				1,498.60
May 6	Balance b/d		443.60				

Alternative Ledger Presentation

It has become acceptable to present ledger accounts in a continous form rather than in the traditional two-sided form. This is the layout used by computer packages when presenting accounts. You may present your ledger accounts in either form. The example in this chapter is presented below in continous form. As you will see, the continous format has a debit column, a credit column and a balance column. The balance column is maintained throughout the month, thus your account is automatically balanced at the end of the month. This is referred to as self-balancing.

In self-balancing ledger accounts you add debit entries to debit balances and you subtract credit entries from debit balances. If the balance is a credit balance, you add credit entries and subtract debit entries to give the balance figure. You need to watch for debit balances becoming credit balances as in the Bank a/c below: on May 6th the debit entry of £1,498.60 converts the £1,055.00 credit balance to a debit balance, i.e. you are adding a +£1,498.60 to a −£1,055.00.

Example continued

How would you post the figures from the previous example in a continuous form?

Solution

General Ledger

Date	Details	F	Debit (£)	Credit (£)	Balance (£)
	Cash a/c				
May 1	Bal b/d				400.00dr
May 6	Payments	cb		371.80	28.20dr
	Bank a/c				
May 1	Bal b/d				550.00cr
May 6	Payments	cb		505.00	1,055.00cr
May 6	Receipts	cb	1,498.60		443.60dr
	Sales a/c				
May 4	Bank	cb		660.00	660.00cr
	VAT a/c				
May 4	Purchases	cb	16.80		16.80dr
May 4	Sales	cb		138.60	121.80cr
	Wages a/c				
May 2	Cash	cb	180.00		180.00dr
	Advertising a/c				
May 2	Bank	cb	120.00		120.00dr
	Purchases a/c				
May 2	Cash	cb	80.00		80.00dr
	Rent a/c				
May 6	Bank	cb	320.00		320.00dr

Debtors Ledger

Date	Details	F	Debit (£)	Credit (£)	Balance (£)
May 4	**E. Moore a/c**			700.00	700.00cr
	Bank	cb			

Creditors Ledger

Date	Details	F	Debit (£)	Credit (£)	Balance (£)
May 2	**D. Smith a/c**		65.00		65.00dr
	Bank	cb			
May 6	**C. Cooke a/c**		95.00		95.00dr
	Bank	cb			

Short Questions

Complete each of the following.

1. A debit opening balance in cash means _____

_____

_____

2. What is a bank overdraft? _____

_____

_____

3. Where is an opening bank overdraft shown? _____

_____

_____

4. Goods sold stating 'VAT inclusive' means that _____

_____

_____

5. Explain 'debtors'. _____

_____

_____

6. Explain 'creditors'. _____

_____

_____

7. Why are folios used? _____

_____

_____

Questions

In each of the following questions the analysis columns are as follows.

      Receipts: Cash, Bank, Sales, VAT, Debtors, Other

      Payments: Cheq. no., Cash, Bank, Purchases, VAT, Creditors, Other

You are asked to write up the analysed cash book (or alternative method) and to post to the ledgers.

Q1. Jan 1   Cash on hand £900; Cash in bank £1,550.

  Jan 2   Purchased goods £330 + VAT @ 21% Cheq. no. 10; Paid rent £120 cash.

  Jan 3   D. Dunne paid £395 by cheque lodged; Cash sales £440 + VAT @ 21%.

  Jan 5   Paid wages £460 Cheq. no. 11; E. Earle paid £60 cash.

  Jan 6   Paid advertising £80 cash; Paid F. Flynn £230 Cheq. no. 12.

Q2. Feb 10 Cash on hand £300; Cash in bank £440.

  Feb 11 Paid G. Green £650 Cheq. no. 31; Paid rent £280 cash.

  Feb 12 H. Holmes paid £60 cash; Cash sales lodged £230 + VAT @ 21%; Purchases £550 + VAT @ 21% by Cheq. no. 32.

  Feb 14 Paid travel expenses £60 cash.

  Feb 16 J. Joyce paid £365 cash.

Q3. Mar 1   Cash on hand £190; Bank overdraft £630.

  Mar 2   Cash sales lodged £900 + VAT @ 21%; Paid wages £230 by Cheq. no. 21.

  Mar 3   K. King paid £230 by cheque; Paid rent £160 cash.

  Mar 4   Purchased goods £510 + VAT @ 21% by Cheq. no. 22; Paid L. Lyons £75 by Cheq. no. 23.

Q4. Apr 1   Cash on hand £290; Cash in bank £1,650.

  Apr 5   Paid M. Murphy £660 by Cheq. no. 1; Purchased goods for £90 cash + VAT @ 21%.

  Apr 6   Paid office expenses £60 by Cheq. no. 2; N. Nolan paid £650 by cheque lodged.

  Apr 7   Sold goods £680 + VAT @ 21% money lodged; Paid wages £90 cash.

  Apr 8   Paid rent £180 by Cheq. no. 3.

Q5. May 1   Cash on hand £460; Cash in bank £2,300.

  May 2   Purchases £800 + VAT @ 21% by Cheq. no. 31; P. Peters paid £500 cash; Paid £310 advertising by Cheq. no. 32.

  May 4   Sold goods £580 cash + VAT @ 21%; Purchased filing cabinet £120 by Cheq. no. 33.

  May 5   Paid Q. Quinn £600 by Cheq. no. 34; Purchased goods £210 + VAT @ 21% by Cheq. no. 35.

  May 6   Lodged £800 cash in bank.

Q6. June 1 Cash on hand £530; Cash in bank £968.

  June 2 Sold goods £330 + VAT @ 21% money lodged; Paid wages £290 cash.

  June 3 R. Ryan paid £230 cash; Purchased goods £605 by Cheq. no. 41, with VAT @ 21% already included in purchase price.

  June 4 Paid wages £160 by Cheq. no. 42; Paid S. Styles £95 cash; T. Traynor paid £650 by cheque.

  June 6 Lodged £300 cash in bank.

Chapter 3

Petty Cash Book

The petty cash book (pcb) is used to record small office expenses for which it would be inconvenient and wasteful to be writing cheques. There is usually one person in each office in charge of petty cash and all payments must be signed for by this person. Numbered vouchers are used to record the amount paid and what it was spent on. Petty cash books are kept on the **Imprest System**. This means that each week or month the person in charge begins with the same amount. They are reimbursed from 'bank' for what they spend. This is referred to as restoring the Imprest. As in the main cash book, analysis columns are kept to classify expenses. Underneath each analysis column should be a folio indicating where the double entry can be found. Petty cash books can be kept weekly, fortnightly or monthly depending on what is appropriate for the business.

Example

Aug 1   Petty cash balance £60.

Aug 2   Paid taxi £10.20 Voucher no. 1; Cleaning £6 Voucher no. 2.

Aug 3   Paid for postage stamps £3.20 Voucher no. 3; Bus fare £2.20 Voucher no. 4.

Aug 4   Bought typing paper £6.50 Voucher no. 5; Paid for flowers £4.50 Voucher no. 6; Paid parcel post £10.20 Voucher no. 7.

Aug 6   Gave donation £1.50 to local charity Voucher no. 8; Bought envelopes £1.80 Voucher no. 9.

Aug 7   Paid for window cleaning £5.40 Voucher no. 10.

You are asked to record these expenses in the petty cash book with five analysis columns: Postage, Stationery, Travel, Cleaning and Sundries. Then balance off the petty cash book and restore the Imprest.

Solution

Petty Cash Book

Date	Details	(£)	Date	Details	V. no.	Total (£)	Post (£)	Stat (£)	Trav (£)	Clean (£)	Sund (£)
Aug 1	Balance	60.00	Aug 2	Taxi	1	10.20			10.20		
Aug 2				Cleaning	2	6.00				6.00	
Aug 3				Postage	3	3.20	3.20				
Aug 3				Bus fare	4	2.20			2.20		
Aug 4				Typing paper	5	6.50		6.50			
Aug 4				Flowers	6	4.50					4.50
Aug 4				Parcel post	7	10.20	10.20				
Aug 6				Donation	8	1.50					1.50
Aug 6				Envelopes	9	1.80		1.80			
Aug 7				Window cl.	10	5.40				5.40	
Aug 7				Balance c/d		8.50					
		60.00				60.00	13.40	8.30	12.40	11.40	6.00
Aug 7	Bal b/d	8.50					gl	gl	gl	gl	gl
Aug 7	Cheque	51.50*									

* The double entry for this can be found in the cash book.

Rules for Posting

Each analysis total is posted to the relevant general ledger account. There is no need to post each individual entry. In the example all the entries are credits in the petty cash book, so they are debits in the ledger.

General Ledger

Debit Date	Details	F	(£)	Date	Details	F	Credit (£)
			Postage a/c				
Aug 7	Petty cash	pcb	13.40				
			Stationery a/c				
Aug 7	Petty cash	pcb	8.30				
			Travel a/c				
Aug 7	Petty cash	pcb	12.40				
			Cleaning a/c				
Aug 7	Petty cash	pcb	11.40				
			Sundries a/c				
Aug 7	Petty cash	pcb	6.00				

Short Questions

1. What is a petty cash book used to record? _____
   _____
   _____

2. Why must petty cash vouchers be signed? _____
   _____
   _____

3. What does the Imprest System mean?_____
   _____
   _____

4. You are given an opening balance of £100. You spend £79.65 during the month. How much is
   needed to restore the Imprest? _____
   _____
   _____

5. You are in charge of petty cash in the office. You are asked to complete the petty cash voucher using today's date for £3.95 paid for a taxi.

PETTY CASH VOUCHER
No. 45
Signed   Date

6. You receive a cheque for £65.60 from the bookkeeper at the end of May. State below how this would have been recorded in the cash book. _____

_____

_____

7. Why must the petty cash vouchers be in numerical order?_____

_____

_____

Questions

In each of the following questions complete the petty cash book, using the following five analysis columns: Postage, Travel, Stationery, Cleaning, Sundries. Post the petty cash book to the ledgers.

Q1. Sept 1   Bal £70.
     Sept 3   Paid bus fare £3.20 V. no. 21; Flowers £5.50 V. no. 22; Parcel post £3.80 V. no. 23.
     Sept 8   Paid £4.50 for window cleaning V. no. 24.
     Sept 9   Postage paid £6.60 V. no. 25; Birthday cake bought £3.90 V. no. 26.
     Sept 13   Paid taxi fares £10.80 V. no. 27.
     Sept 18   Paid office cleaning £12.50 V. no. 28.
     Sept 19   Paid £6.80 for envelopes V. no. 29.
     Sept 24   Paid £1.80 to register letter V. no. 30.
     Sept 28   Bought writing pads £4.50 V. no. 31.
     Sept 30   Received cheque from bank to restore the Imprest.

Q2. Oct 1   Bal £50.

  Oct 2   Paid £6.80 for typing paper V. no. 40; Paid cleaning £6.80 V. no. 41.

  Oct 3   Bought raffle ticket £1 V. no. 42; Paid for postage stamps £5.60 V. no. 43.

  Oct 4   Paid for birthday present £6.60 V. no. 44; Paid bus fares £3.60 V. no. 45.

  Oct 5   Paid £3.80 for envelopes V. no. 46; £1.60 was paid for tea and coffee V. no. 47.

  Oct 6   Taxi fare £9.50 paid V. no. 48; Drawing paper bought £2.30 V. no. 49.

  Oct 7   Received cheque to restore the Imprest.

Q3. Nov 1   Bal £200.

  Nov 3   Paid £3.60 for coffee and milk V. no. 50; Paid £1.80 bus fares V. no. 51; parcel post £6.60 V. no. 52.

  Nov 5   Paid £10.50 cleaning V. no. 53; Paid £9.80 for note paper V. no. 54.

  Nov 10   Taxi fare paid £12.60 V. no. 55; Flowers for reception £6.00 V. no. 56.

  Nov 15   Paid £15 for carpet cleaning V. no. 57; Paid bus fares £4.80 V. no. 58.

  Nov 18   Registered a letter £3.20 V. no. 59; Tea and coffee bought £4.80 V. no. 60.

  Nov 23   Paid £6.20 for envelopes V. no. 61; Printing cartridge bought £18 V. no. 62.

  Nov 28   Paid bus fares £3.20 V. no. 63; Felt tip pens bought £4.90 V. no. 64.

  Nov 29   Received cheque to restore the Imprest.

Q4. Dec 1   Bal £80.

  Dec 2   Xmas cards £2.50 were bought V. no. 30.

  Dec 3   Taxi fare paid £5 V. no. 31; Donation to charity £5 V. no. 32.

  Dec 4   Envelopes bought £7 V. no. 33; Paid for Xmas decorations £4.20 V. no. 34.

  Dec 5   Paid bus fares £1.95 V. no. 35; Paid window cleaning £5.50 V. no. 36; Paid for manilla folders £6.10 V. no. 37.

  Dec 6   Paid £8.10 for postage stamps V. no. 38; Paid courier £20 V. no. 39.

  Dec 7   Received cheque to restore the Imprest.

Chapter 4

Purchases Day Book

The purchases day book (pdb) is used to record all purchases of goods made by a business on credit, where 'purchasing on credit' means buying goods but not paying for them until a later date. The purchases day book contains a list of all the people from whom goods were purchased on credit. These are the creditors of the business. The business owes them money.

The purchases day book is written up from invoices that the business has received. An **INVOICE** gives details about the goods, unit price, VAT, total price and any terms of sale. The cost before VAT, the VAT and the invoice total are shown in the purchases day book. The purchases day book is used only for purchases of goods on credit. Purchases of a fixed asset on credit are recorded in the general journal so they should be ignored at this stage.

Procedures for Recording Credit Purchases

1. Write up the day book in chronological order from the invoices received.
2. Post to ledgers.

   Credit the Creditors a/c with the total amount owed, i.e. including VAT

   Debit the Purchases a/c with the total amount before VAT

   Debit the VAT a/c with the total of the VAT column

Example
From the following, write up the purchases day book and post to the ledgers.

May 1 Bought goods on credit from D. Mc Garry Inv. no. 106, £1,000 + VAT @ 21%.

May 3 Bought goods on credit from J. Mc Govern Inv. no. 6315, £510 + VAT @ 21%.

May 6 Received Inv. no. 318 for £ 480 + VAT @ 21% from S. Mc Guinness.

Solution

	Purchases Day Book	F	Purch (£)	VAT (£)	Total (£)
May 1	D. McGarry Inv. no. 106	cl	1,000	210.00	1,210.00
May 3	J. Mc Govern Inv. no. 6315	cl	510	107.10	617.10
May 6	S. McGuinness Inv. no. 318	cl	480	100.80	580.80
			£1,990	417.90	2,407.90
			gl	gl	

Rules for Posting

The purchases day book contains a list of all the credit purchases. We now need to post these to the ledgers. There are two sides to each transaction.

1. The business owes the creditor money, shown on the credit side of the creditors account.
2. The business received goods, i.e. made purchases, shown on the debit side of the purchases and VAT a/cs in the general ledger. The VAT a/c is required by the revenue commissioners to show the amount owing to them.
3. As before folios are used to show where the double entry can be found.

| Debit | | | | General Ledger | | | | Credit |
Date	Details	F	(£)	Date	Details	F	(£)

Purchases a/c

Date	Details	F	(£)	Date	Details	F	(£)
May 6	Sundries as per purchases day book	pdb	1,990.00				

VAT a/c

Date	Details	F	(£)	Date	Details	F	(£)
May 6	Cr purch	pdb	417.90				

Creditors Ledger
D. McGarry a/c

Date	Details	F	(£)	Date	Details	F	(£)
				May 1	Purch	pdb	1,210.00

J. McGovern a/c

Date	Details	F	(£)	Date	Details	F	(£)
				May 3	Purch	pdb	617.10

S. McGuinness a/c

Date	Details	F	(£)	Date	Details	F	(£)
				May 6	Purch	pdb	580.80

Short Questions

1. What is an invoice? _____

_____

_____

2. Name five pieces of information contained on the invoice.

   1. _____

   2. _____

   3. _____

   4. _____

   5. _____

3. Explain what a creditor is. _____

_____

_____

4. What is a trade discount?_____

_____

_____

5. What are folios?_____

_____

_____

6. You own a supermarket. Give an example of each of the following:

    1. Goods for resale _____

    2. Fixed asset_____

Questions

In each of the following questions write up the purchases day book and post to the relevant ledgers. Remember to include your folios.

Q1. May 2   Bought on credit from M. Foley Ltd Inv. no. 732 £650 + VAT @ 21%.

     May 3   Purchased on credit from J. Connolly Ltd Inv. no. 5315 £1,650 + VAT @ 21%.

     May 6   Purchased on credit from L. Jackson Ltd Inv. no. 361 £3,650 + VAT @ 21%.

     May 7   Bought on credit from T. Mc Garvey Ltd Inv. no. 316 £65 + VAT @ 21%.

Q2. July 14   Received Inv. no. a316 from J. Brophy Ltd £500 + VAT @ 21%.

     July 16   Received Inv. no. 936 from J. Browne Ltd £963 + VAT @ 21%.

     July 17   Received Inv. no. a326 from J. Brophy Ltd £600 + VAT @ 21%.

Q3. Sept 20   Purchased goods on credit from P. Daly Ltd £70 + VAT @ 21% Inv. no. 106.

     Sept 22   Purchased goods on credit from M. Murphy Ltd £430 + VAT @ 21% Inv. no. 110.

     Sept 24   Bought on credit from R. Rudden Ltd £680 + VAT @ 21% Inv. no. 983.

Q4. Aug 24   Bought goods on credit from E. Toft Ltd £632 + VAT @ 21% Inv. no. 631.

     Aug 26   Purchased goods on credit from D. O'Brien Ltd £847 + VAT @ 21% Inv. no. 314.

     Aug 28   Received Inv. no. 386 from E. Toft Ltd £530 + VAT @ 21%.

Chapter 5

Purchases Returns Day Book

Purchases returns are made when some of the goods previously bought are returned. They are often called 'returns outwards'. A credit note is received by the business to let them know they owe less.

There may be several reasons why goods are returned.

1. Wrong goods sent, subsequently returned.
2. Too many goods sent, extra goods are returned.
3. Damaged goods are returned.

There are occassions other than for returns that credit notes are issued.

1. An allowance is given because some of the goods were damaged.
2. The buyer was overcharged on the original invoice.
3. The buyer returned packaging material previously charged for.

Whether the credit note is received for returns or for another reason the treatment in the books is the same.

Procedure for Recording Purchases Returns

1. Write up the day book in chronological order.
2. Post purchase returns to ledgers.

   Debit the Creditors a/c with the total amount of the reduction

   Credit the Purchases Returns a/c with the total amount from the day book before VAT

   Credit the VAT a/c with the total amount from the day book VAT column

Example

From the following, write up the purchases day book (pdb) and the purchases returns day book (prdb). Post these to the relevant ledgers.

May 1   Bought goods on credit from N. Leigh Ltd Inv. no. 680, £550 + VAT @ 21%.

May 6   Purchased on credit from A. Monks Ltd Inv. no. 6216, £335 + VAT @ 21%.

May 8   Returned goods to N. Leigh Ltd, Credit Note (CN) no. 68, £180 + VAT @ 21%.

Solution

Purchases Day Book

	Purch	F	Purch (£)	VAT (£)	Total (£)
May 1	N. Leigh Ltd Inv. no. 680	cl	550	115.50	665.50
May 6	A. Monks Ltd Inv. no. 6216	cl	335	70.35	405.35
			885	185.85	1,070.85
			gl	gl	

Purchases Returns Day Book

	Purch. Ret.	F	P Ret (£)	VAT (£)	Total (£)
May 8	N. Leigh Ltd CN no. 68	cl	180	37.80	217.80
			gl	gl	

Rules for Posting

The purchases day book has already been posted, so we want to record the purchases returns.
1. The business owes the creditor less money, shown on the debit side of the creditors account.
2. The business sent back goods, i.e made purchases returns. The total of the purchases returns column is shown on the credit side of the purchases returns a/c and the total of the VAT column is shown on the credit side of the VAT a/c.

General Ledger

Debit				Credit			
Date	**Details**	**F**	**(£)**	**Date**	**Details**	**F**	**(£)**

Purchases a/c

Date	Details	F	(£)	Date	Details	F	(£)
May 8	Sundries as per purchases daybook	prdb	885.00				

Purchases Returns a/c

Date	Details	F	(£)	Date	Details	F	(£)
				May 8	Sundries as per purchases returns day book	prdb	180

Debit					General Ledger			Credit	
Date	**Details**	**F**	**(£)**	**Date**	**Details**		**F**	**(£)**	

VAT a/c

	Cr Purch	prdb	185.85	May 8	P Returns		prdb	37.80
				May 8	Balance		c/d	148.05
			185.85					185.85
May 8	Bal b/d		148.05					

Creditors Ledger*
N. Leigh Ltd a/c

May 8	P Returns	prdb	217.80	May 1	Purchases		pdb	665.50
May 8	Balance c/d		447.70					
			665.50					665.50
				May 8	Balance b/d			447.70

A. Monks Ltd a/c

| | | | | May 6 | Purch | | pdb | 405.35 |

* In the creditors ledger, the credit side is for when the business owes more and the debit side is for when the business owes less.

Short Questions

1. For what reason are credit notes received? _____
_____
_____

2. Give another name for purchases returns. _____

3. Why might goods be returned? _____
_____
_____

4. What information is contained on a credit note?_____
_____
_____

5. What should be done with credit notes received? _____
_____
_____

Questions

In each of the following questions write up the purchases day book, purchases returns day book and post to the ledgers. Remember to fill in the folios.

Q1. May 6   Received Inv. no. 368 from B. Brady Ltd £386 + VAT @ 21%.

     May 7   Bought on credit from C. Crowley Ltd Inv. no. 426 goods for £835 + VAT @ 21%.

     May 8   Returned goods to B. Brady Ltd CN no. 93 £135 + VAT @ 21%.

     May 13   Returned goods to C. Crowley Ltd CN no. 136 £310 + VAT @ 21%.

Q2. July 20   Bought on credit from D. Daly Ltd Inv. no. 513 goods £736 + VAT @ 21%.

     July 22   Bought on credit from E. Enright Ltd Inv. no. 1836 cost £2,500 + VAT @ 21%.

     July 26   Returned goods to D. Daly Ltd CN no. 86 £340 + VAT @ 21%.

     July 27   Bought on credit from F. Flood Ltd Inv. no. 6346 £1,600 + VAT @ 21%.

Q3. Sept 14   Received Inv. no. 6316 from G. Graham Ltd £1,680 + VAT @ 21%.

     Sept 16   Received Inv. no. 5638 from H. Horan Ltd £980 + VAT @ 21%.

     Sept 18   Received CN no. 416 from G. Graham Ltd £550 + VAT @ 21%.

     Sept 19   Received Inv. no. 7181 from I. Irwan Ltd £3,680 + VAT @ 21%.

     Sept 21   Received CN no. 83 from H. Horan Ltd £95 + VAT @ 21%.

     Sept 21   Received Inv. no. 6356 from G. Graham Ltd £1,900 + VAT @ 21%.

Q4. Aug 2   Purchased on credit from K. Kirwan Ltd Inv. no. 763, £4,180 + VAT @ 21%.

     Aug 4   Bought on credit from L. Lee Ltd Inv. no. 836 £1,850 + VAT @ 21%.

     Aug 6   Returned goods to L. Lee Ltd CN no. 56 £460 + VAT @ 21%.

     Aug 7   Purchased goods from M. May Ltd Inv. no. 186 £900 + VAT @ 21%.

     Aug 8   Returned goods to K. Kirwan Ltd CN no. 98 £1,260 + VAT @ 21%.

     Aug 9   Purchased goods from L. Lee Ltd Inv. no. 860 £700 + VAT @ 21%.

Chapter 6

Sales Day Book

The sales day book (sdb) is used to record sales on credit. It is a list of people to whom the business sold on credit. 'Sales on credit' refers to goods (stock) sold by the business for payment in the future. The customers who owe the money are called debtors of the business.

Granting Credit

A business will not sell to all its customers on credit. A customer must be creditworthy to be granted credit. Creditworthiness means that the customer has a good track record for paying bills when they are due. The business can check out the creditworthiness of a potential customer by:

1. asking for a bank reference,
2. asking for a trade reference,
3. checking their own accounts to see if they had business with that potential customer in the past,
4. using a credit status investigation agency.

If a firm sells on credit, it must have a good credit control system. This is to ensure that debtors pay on time and that they do not exceed their credit limit. A business will have a policy of allowing a certain length of time for their debtors to pay, for example only giving 1 month of credit. They will also set a credit limit for each debtor.

The sales day book is written up from invoices sent. The cost before VAT, the VAT and the invoice total are shown.

The sales day book is only used for the sale of goods on credit. Fixed assets sold on credit are not included here.

Procedure for Recording Credit Sales

1. Write up the day book in chronological order.
2. Post to ledgers.

    Debit the Debtors a/c with total owed to business

    Credit the Sales a/c with the total amount from the sales day book before VAT

    Credit the VAT a/c with the total from the sales day book VAT column

Example

From the following, write up the sales day book and post to the ledgers.

May 1   Sold goods on credit to P. Power Ltd Inv. no. 631 £686 + VAT @ 21%.

May 2   Sent invoice to Q. Quinn Ltd Inv. no. 632 £834 + VAT @ 21%.

May 4   Sold on credit to R. Rice Ltd Inv. no. 633 £1,460 + VAT @ 21%.

Solution

Date	Sales Day Book	F	Sales (£)	VAT (£)	Total (£)
May 1	P. Power Ltd Inv. no. 631	dl	686	144.06	830.06
May 2	Q. Quinn Ltd Inv. no. 632	dl	834	175.14	1,009.14
May 4	R. Rice Ltd Inv. no. 633	dl	1,460	306.60	1,766.60
			2,980	625.80	3,605.80
			gl	gl	

Debtors Ledger

Debit   P. Power Ltd a/c   **Credit**

Date	Details	F	(£)	Date	Details	F	(£)
May 1	Sales	sdb	830.06				

Q. Quinn Ltd a/c

Date	Details	F	(£)	Date	Details	F	(£)
May 2	Sales	sdb	1,009.14				

R. Rice Ltd a/c

Date	Details	F	(£)	Date	Details	F	(£)
May 4	Sales	sdb	1,766.60				

General Ledger

Sales a/c

				Date	Details	F	(£)
				May 4	Sundries as per sales day book	sdb	2,980.00

VAT a/c

				Date	Details	F	(£)
				May 4	Cr sales	sdb	625.80

Short Questions

Q1. For what reason is an invoice sent? _____

_____

Q2. Who is a debtor?_____

Q3. What does a debit balance b/d on a debtors a/c mean? _____

_____

Q4. How would a business decide to whom they would sell on credit?_____

_____

_____

_____

Questions

In each of the following questions write up the sales day book and post to the ledgers.

Q1. Aug 1   Sold on credit to M. Murphy Ltd Inv. no. 736, £1,650 + VAT @ 21%.

Aug 3   Sold on credit to N. Neary Ltd Inv. no. 737 £2,650 + VAT @ 21%.

Aug 5   Sold on credit to O. Orwell Ltd Inv. no. 738 £900 + VAT @ 21%.

Aug 7   Sold on credit to M. Murphy Ltd Inv. no. 739 £1,650 + VAT @ 21%.

Q2. Sept 7   Sent Inv. no. 1063 to P. Pierce Ltd £600 + VAT @ 21%.

Sept 9   Sent Inv. no. 1064 to Q. Quigley Ltd £1,800 + VAT @ 21%.

Sept 10   Sent Inv. no. 1065 to R. Redmond £960 + VAT @ 21%.

Sept 12   Sent Inv. no. 1066 to Q. Quigley Ltd £1,950 + VAT @ 21%.

Q3. Oct 1   Sold on credit to S. Shine Ltd Inv. no. 861 £7,000 + VAT @ 21%.

Oct 3   Sold on credit to T. Traynor Ltd Inv. no. 862 £565 + VAT @ 21%.

Oct 4   Sold on credit to U. Ulman Ltd Inv. no. 863 £487 + VAT @ 21%.

Oct 5   Sent Inv. no. 864 to S. Shine Ltd £689 + VAT @ 21%.

Oct 7   Sent Inv. no. 865 to U. Ulman Ltd £900 + VAT @ 21%.

Q4. Nov 1   Sold on credit to A. Brady Ltd Inv. no. 1063 £960 + VAT @ 21%.

Nov 3   Sold on credit to C. Dunne Ltd Inv. no. 1064 £1,900+ VAT @ 21%.

Nov 4   Sold on credit to A. Brady Ltd Inv. no. 1065 £1,100 + VAT @ 21%.

Nov 6   Sold on credit to E. Flynn Ltd Inv. no. 1066 £3,680 + VAT @ 21%.

Nov 7   Sold on credit to C. Dunne Ltd Inv. no. 1067 £863 + VAT @ 21%.

Chapter 7

Sales Returns Day Book

The sales returns day book (srdb) is used to record sales returns. These occur when customers return goods to the business. These are also known as returns inwards. Cash customers may be given a cash refund. Credit customers (debtors) are issued a credit note which gives details of the goods returned, the price excluding VAT, the VAT and the total. A credit note tells the customer that they owe less. The invoices and credit notes are referred to as 'source documents' used to write up the books.

Procedure for Recording Sales Returns

1. Write up the sales and sales returns books in chronological order.
2. Post to the ledger.

   Credit the Debtors a/c with the total figure from the day book showing a reduction in the amount owed

   Debit the Sales Returns a/c with the total from the sales returns day book before VAT

   Debit the VAT a/c with the total from the sales returns day book VAT column

Example

From the following, write up the sales day book, the sales returns day book and post to the relevant ledgers.

May 1   Sold on credit to I. Jackson Ltd Inv. no. 638 £800 + VAT @ 21%.

May 2   Sold on credit to K. Lee Ltd Inv. no. 639 £1,680 + VAT @ 21%.

May 4   I. Jackson Ltd returned goods; CN no. 118 sent, £190 + VAT @ 21%.

May 5   K. Lee Ltd returned goods, CN no. 119 sent £480 + VAT @ 21%.

Solution

Sales Day Book

Date	Details	F	Sales (£)	VAT (£)	Total (£)
May 1	I. Jackson Ltd Inv. no. 638	dl	800	168.00	968.00
May 2	K. Lee Ltd Inv. no. 639	dl	1,680	352.80	2,032.80
			2,480	520.80	3,000.80
			gl	gl	

30

Sales Returns Day Book

Date	Details	F	S Ret (£)	VAT (£)	Total (£)
May 4	I. Jackson Ltd CN no. 118	dl	190	39.90	229.90
May 2	K. Lee Ltd CN no. 119	dl	480	100.80	580.80
			670	140.70	810.70
			gl	gl	

Debtors Ledger

Debit   **I. Jackson Ltd a/c**   **Credit**

Date	Details	F	(£)	Date	Details	F	(£)
May 1	Sales	sdb	968.00	May 4	S Ret	srdb	229.90
				May 5	Bal b/d		738.10
			968.00				968.00
May 5	Bal b/d		738.10				

K. Lee Ltd a/c

Date	Details	F	(£)	Date	Details	F	(£)
May 2	Sales	sdb	2,032.80	May 5	S Returns	srdb	580.80
				May 5	Bal c/d		1,452.00
			2,032.80				2,032.80
May 5	Bal b/d		1,452.00				

General Ledger

Debit   **Sales a/c**   **Credit**

Date	Details	F	(£)	Date	Details	F	(£)
				May 5	Sundries as per sales day book	sdb	2,480.00

VAT a/c

Date	Details	F	(£)	Date	Details	F	(£)
May 5	S Ret	srdb	140.70	May 5	Cr Sales	sdb	520.80
May 5	Bal c/d		380.10				
			520.80				520.80
				May 5	Balance b/d		380.10

Sales Returns a/c

Date	Details	F	(£)				
May 5	Sundries as per sales returns day book	srdb	670.00				

Short Questions

1. State two reasons why sales returns might arise.

   1. _____

   2. _____

2. How are sales returns recorded? _____

_____

_____

_____

3. What affect have sales returns on a debtors account? _____

_____

_____

_____

4. How might a business check the creditworthiness of a potential customer? _____

_____

_____

5. Why is credit control important for a business? _____

_____

_____

_____

Questions

In each of the following questions, write up the sales day book and sales returns day book, and post to the ledgers.

Q1. Nov 1   Sold on credit to Mooney Ltd Inv. no. 836 £685 + VAT @ 21%.

Nov 2   Sold on credit to Neary Ltd Inv. no. 837 £765 + VAT @ 21%.

Nov 3   Sold on credit to Price Ltd Inv. no. 838 £1,650 + VAT @ 21%.

Nov 5   Neary Ltd returned goods £550 + VAT @ 21%; CN no. 136 sent.

Nov 7   Price Ltd returned goods £300 + VAT @ 21%; CN no. 137 sent.

Q2. Dec 7   Sent Inv. no. 83 to Redmond Ltd £600 + VAT @ 21%.

Dec 8   Sent Inv. no. 84 to Skelly Ltd £1,960 + VAT @ 21%.

Dec 11   Redmond Ltd returned goods £180 + VAT @ 21%; CN no. 63 sent.

Dec 13   Sent Inv. no. 85 to Skelly Ltd £140 + VAT @ 21%.

Dec 14   Skelly Ltd returned goods £100 + VAT @ 21%; CN no. 64 sent.

Q3. Jan 21   Sold on credit to Tuohy Ltd Inv. no. 836 £3,900 + VAT @ 21%.

Jan 22   Sold on credit to Vickers Ltd Inv. no. 837 £1,600 + VAT @ 21%.

Jan 23   Tuohy Ltd returned goods; CN no. 33 sent £360 + VAT @ 21%.

Jan 24   Sold on credit to Wallis Ltd £650 + VAT @ 21%; Inv. no. 838 sent.

Jan 26   Vickers Ltd returned goods £700 + VAT @ 21%; CN no. 34 sent.

Q4. Feb 21   Sent Inv. no. 186 to Apple Ltd £5,000 + VAT @ 21%.

Feb 22   Apple Ltd returned goods; CN no. 70 sent £2,500 + VAT @ 21%.

Feb 24   Sold on credit to Bean Ltd Inv. no. 187 £650 + VAT @ 21%.

Feb 26   Sold on credit to Crow Ltd Inv. no. 188 sent £1,680 + VAT @ 21%.

Feb 27   Bean Ltd returned goods £310 + VAT @ 21%; CN no. 71 sent.

Chapter 8

Trial Balance

The trial balance is a list of all the closing balances in the cash books and ledgers, i.e. debtors balances, creditors balances, general ledger balances, cash book and petty cash book balances. The trial balance is not part of the double-entry system. It is a control mechanism, i.e. a way of checking that all the debit entries match the credit entries. We are using a system of double entry so everything has been entered twice: once on the debit side and once on the credit side of a ledger account.

Procedures for Recording in the Trial Balance

1. List all debit balances brought down in the debit column.
2. List all credit balances brought down in the credit column.

Note. If there is only one entry in an account, then this is the closing balance to be transferred to the trial balance.

The trial balance is usually prepared monthly and is a control mechanism, i.e. errors may arise causing a difference between the columns. The difference may be entered in a suspense account until the cause of the error(s) can be found.

Errors may arise because

1. an item may not have been posted to the ledger,
2. an incorrect amount may have been posted,
3. the totals in the day books may have been incorrect hence the relevant ledger accounts will be incorrect,
4. an entry may be posted to the incorrect side of the ledger account.

Errors not shown by the trial balance

Other errors may have been made that do not show up on the trial balance, i.e. the trial balance still balances. Can you give examples of this?

1. _____

2. _____

3. _____

Example

From the following, write up the day books, post to the ledgers and extract a trial balance on August 31.

Aug 2   Sold on credit to Noonan Ltd £760 + VAT @ 21% Inv. no. 831.

Aug 3   Received Inv. no. 305 from Orpen Ltd £650 + VAT @ 21%.

Aug 7   Sold on credit to Peters Ltd £8,800 + VAT @ 21% Inv. no. 832.

Aug 13   Noonan Ltd returned goods £100 + VAT @ 21%; CN no. 68 sent.

Aug 14   Purchased on credit from Ryan Ltd £3,680 + VAT @ 21% Inv. no. 388.

Aug 18   Returned goods to Orpen Ltd £280 + VAT @ 21%; CN no. 18 sent.

Aug 19   Sold on credit to Richards Ltd £6,800 + VAT @ 21% Inv. no. 833.

Aug 28   Sent CN no. 69 to Peters Ltd £1,200 + VAT @ 21%.

Solution

Purchases Day Book

Date	Details	F	Purch (£)	VAT (£)	Total (£)
Aug 3	Orpen Ltd Inv. no. 305	cl	650	136.50	786.50
Aug 14	Ryan Ltd Inv. no. 388	cl	3,680	772.80	4,452.80
		£	4,330	909.30	5,239.30
			gl	gl	

Purchases Returns Day Book

Date	Details	F	P Rets (£)	VAT (£)	Total (£)
Aug 18	Orpen Ltd CN no. 18	cl	280	58.80	338.80
			gl	gl	

Sales Day Book

Date	Details	F	Sales (£)	VAT (£)	Total (£)
Aug 2	Noonan Ltd Inv. no. 831	dl	760	159.60	919.60
Aug 7	Peters Ltd Inv. no. 832	dl	8,800	1,848.00	10,648.00
Aug 19	Richards Ltd Inv. no. 833	dl	6,800	1,428.00	8,228.00
		£	16,360	3,435.60	19,795.60
			gl	gl	

Sales Returns Day Book

Date	Details	F	S Rets (£)	VAT (£)	Total (£)
Aug 13	Noonan Ltd CN no. 68	dl	100	21.00	121.00
Aug 28	Peters Ltd CN no. 69	dl	1,200	252.00	1,452.00
		£	1,300	273.00	1,573.00
			gl	gl	

Balance off each of the accounts below yourself.

Creditors Ledger

Debit   Orpen Ltd a/c   **Credit**

Date	Details	F	(£)	Date	Details	F	(£)
Aug 18	P Ret	prdb	338.80	Aug 3	Purch	pdb	786.50

Ryan Ltd a/c

Date	Details	F	(£)	Date	Details	F	(£)
				Aug 14	Purch	pdb	4,452.80

Debtors ledger

Noonan Ltd a/c

Date	Details	F	(£)	Date	Details	F	(£)
Aug 2	Sales	sdb	919.60	Aug 13	S Ret	srdb	121.00

Peters Ltd a/c

Date	Details	F	(£)	Date	Details	F	(£)
Aug 7	Sales	sdb	10,648.00	Aug 28	S Ret	srdb	1,452.00

Richards Ltd a/c

Date	Details	F	(£)	Date	Details	F	(£)
Aug 19	Sales	sdb	8,228.00				

General ledger

Debit   **Purchases a/c**   **Credit**

Date	Details	F	(£)	Date	Details	F	(£)
Aug 31	Sundries as per purchases day book	pdb	4,330.00				

Purchases Returns a/c

Date	Details	F	(£)	Date	Details	F	(£)
				Aug 31	Sundries as per purchases returns day book	prdb	280.00

Sales a/c

Date	Details	F	(£)	Date	Details	F	(£)
				Aug 31	Sundries	sb	16,360

Sales Returns a/c

Date	Details	F	(£)	Date	Details	F	(£)
Aug 31	Sundries	srdb	1,300				

VAT a/c

Date	Details	F	(£)	Date	Details	F	(£)
Aug 31	Cr Pur	pdb	909.30	Aug 31	P Ret	prdb	58.80
Aug 31	S Ret	srdb	273.00	Aug 31	Cr Sales	sdb	3,435.60

Complete the Trial Balance below.

Trial balance as at August 31

	F	Debit (£)	Credit (£)
Creditors			
Orpen Ltd	cl		
Ryan Ltd	cl		
Debtors			
Noonan Ltd			
Peters Ltd			
Richards Ltd			
Purchases a/c			
P Returns a/c			
Sales a/c			
S Returns a/c			
VAT a/c			

Both sides should add up to the same amount showing that the trial balance balances.

Short Questions

1. Accounts showing money owed to suppliers are recorded in the _____ ledger.

2. The trial balance is part of double entry?

  True   _____
  False   _____

3. The trial balance will always balance?

  True   _____
  False   _____

4. Give three reasons why a trial balance might not balance?

  1. _____

  2. _____

  3. _____

5. What is a suspense account? _____

  _____

  _____

Questions

In each of the following questions, write up the day book, post to the relevant ledgers and extract a trial balance. Remember to fill in your folios.

Q1. May 1   Sold on credit to Green Ltd Inv. no. 123 £1,000 + VAT @ 21%.

May 3   Bought on credit from Brown Ltd goods for £387 + VAT @ 21% Inv. no. 789.

May 5   Sold on credit to Black Ltd goods £9,650 + VAT @ 21%; Inv. no. 124 sent.

May 6   Returned goods to Brown Ltd £160 + VAT @ 21%; CN no. 68 sent.

May 7   Bought from White Ltd goods £600 + VAT @ 21%; Inv. no. 736 received.

May 7   Sold on credit to Grey Ltd goods £180 + VAT @ 21%; Inv. no. 125 sent.

Q2. June 7   Purchased on credit from Amber Ltd goods £480 + VAT @ 21%; Inv. no. 638 sent.

June 8   Sold on credit to Green Ltd goods £580 + VAT @ 21%; Inv. no. 710 sent.

June 8   Returned goods to Amber Ltd £190 + VAT @ 21%; CN no. 185 received.

June 10   Purchased on credit from Amber Ltd goods £1,500 + VAT @ 21%; Inv. no. 667 received.

June 12   Sold on credit to White Ltd goods £3,650 + VAT @ 21%; Inv. no. 711 sent.

June 14   Green Ltd returned goods £280 + VAT @ 21%; CN no. 86 sent.

Q3. July 8   Sold on credit to Green Ltd goods Inv. no. 85 £8,500 + VAT @ 21%.

July 9   Purchased on credit from Brown Ltd goods £685 + VAT @ 21%; Inv. no. 635 received.

July 9   Green Ltd returned goods £3,600 + VAT @ 21%; CN no. 560 sent.

July 11   Sold on credit to Blue Ltd Inv. no. 86 £680 + VAT @ 21%.

July 12   Bought on credit from Black Ltd £6,850 + VAT @ 21%; Inv. no. 830.

July 14   Blue Ltd returned goods £186 + VAT @ 21%; CN no. 561 sent.

Q4. Aug 7   Sent Inv. no. 681 to White Ltd £600 + VAT @ 21%.

Aug 8   Received Inv. no. 830 from Coral Ltd £3,000 + VAT @ 21%.

Aug 9   Sent CN no. 38 to White Ltd £200 + VAT @ 21%.

Aug 11   Received Inv. no. 930 from Coral Ltd £1,600 + VAT @ 21%.

Aug 12   Sent Debit Note no. 11 to White Ltd £100 + VAT @ 21%.

Aug 13   Sent Inv. no. 682 to Yellow Ltd £800 + VAT @ 21%.

Aug 14   Received CN no. 9 from Coral Ltd £80 + VAT @ 21%.

Aug 14   Sent CN no. 39 to Yellow Ltd £200 + VAT @ 21%.

Chapter 9

Purchase and Sale of an Asset on Credit

The purchase and sale of an asset on credit are sometimes called 'uncommon entries' and refer to business transactions that cannot be recorded in the purchases, sales, purchases returns or sales returns day books as they do not involve the buying or selling of goods on credit. They cannot go into the cash book as no money payment was involved. These entries are recorded in the general journal before being posted to the ledgers.

Example

A van worth £6,000 was sold on credit to M. Nolan on May 5.

Solution

GENERAL JOURNAL

Date	Details	F	Debit (£)	Credit (£)
May 5	M. Nolan	dl	6,000	
	Motor Vehicles	gl		6,000
	Van sold on credit*			

* An explanation is always included for each transaction.

Debtors Ledger

Debit				M. Nolan Ltd			Credit
Date	Details	F	(£)	Date	Details	F	(£)
May 1	Bal c/d		—				
May 5	M Van	gj	6,000				

General Ledger

Debit				Motor vehicles a/c			Credit
Date	Details	F	(£)	Date	Details	F	(£)
May 1	Balance		—	May 5	M. Nolan	gj	6,000

Example

On June 15 filing cabinets were bought on credit from Business Supplies Ltd £450 + 21% VAT.

Solution

GENERAL JOURNAL

Date	Details	F	Debit (£)	Credit (£)
June 15	Office Equipment	gl	450.00	
	VAT	gl	94.50	
	Business Supplies Ltd	dl		544.50
	Filing cabinets bought on credit*			

* An explanation is always included for each transaction.

Complete the posting to the accounts below yourself.

General Ledger

Office Equipment a/c

Date	Details	F	(£)	Date	Details	F	(£)

VAT a/c

Date	Details	F	(£)	Date	Details	F	(£)

Creditors Ledger

Business Supplies Ltd a/c

Date	Details	F	(£)	Date	Details	F	(£)

Questions

Record each of the following in the general journal and post to the relevant ledgers.

Q1. Aug 8   Sold motor car for £3,000 on credit to ABC Ltd.

Q2. Aug 9   Purchased new shop fittings on credit from XYZ Ltd £360 + VAT @ 21%.

Q3. Aug 16 Sold computers on credit to MNN Ltd for £3,000. VAT @ 21% applies.

Q4. Aug 20 Purchased new photocopier on credit from RST Ltd £8,600 + VAT @ 21%.

Chapter 10

Complete Trial Balance Questions Including Control Accounts

In this chapter we bring together all that we have learned in previous chapters. You are asked to record all entries in the books of first entry, i.e. from source documents, complete the posting, balance the accounts and extract a trial balance.

Procedure for Extracting a Trial Balance

1. Write up opening general journal.
2. Write up the uncommon entries if any.
3. Post opening general journal and the uncommon entry.
4. Write up the four day books, i.e. purchases, sales, purchases returns and sales returns.
5. Post the day books to the ledgers.
6. Write up the petty cash book.
7. Post the petty cash book.
8. Write up the analysed cash book.
9. Post the analysed cash book.
10. Balance off any accounts that need balancing and bring down the relevant balance.
11. Extract a trial balance to check the accuracy of your recording.
12. Prepare control accounts.

Use this checklist to help you complete all the parts of the question. Remember to complete the folios and record document numbers as you work through the question. Your work should be neatly presented. Document numbers are relevant to invoices, credit notes, cheques and petty cash vouchers.

Control Accounts

Debtors and creditors control accounts are prepared each month to check the accuracy of the recording. This is important for the business as errors may have occurred in individual debtors and creditors accounts.

The closing balance in the debtors control account should be the same as all the individual debtors closing balances added together.

The closing balance on the creditors control should be the same as the individual creditors closing balances added together.

The control accounts are not part of the double-entry system. A debtors control account looks exactly like an individual debtors account. A creditors control account looks exactly like an individual creditors account.

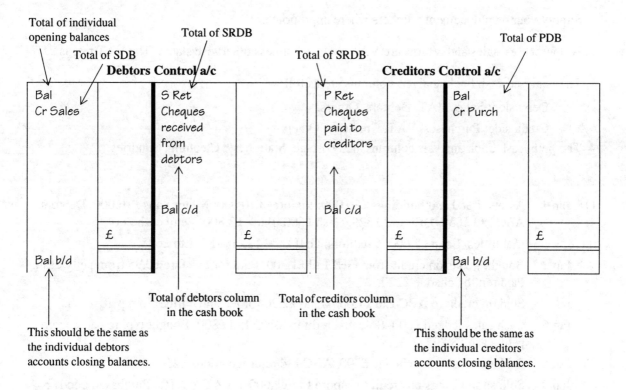

Example

Complete the debtors and creditors control accounts below from the following balances on Sept 30:

> Total payments to creditors £10,100; Total credit sales £14,680; Total credit purchases £11,100; Total sales returns £500; Total purchases returns £1,230; Total receipts from debtors £15,650.

Debtors Control a/c

	£		£
Sept 30 Bal b/d	5,680		
	£		£

Creditors Control a/c

	£		£
		Sept 30 Bal	4,500
	£		£

Questions

Complete each of the following questions to trial balance.

Directions

1. Supply your own document numbers where appropriate.

2. All purchases, sales and returns are VAT exclusive unless otherwise stated. The VAT rate is 21%.

3. The analysed cash book analysis columns are as follows.

      Debit side: Sales, VAT, Debtors, Others.

      Credit side: Purchases, VAT, Creditors, Others.

4. The petty cash book analysis columns are: Postage, Stationery, Cleaning, Sundries.

Q1. Jan 1	Assets: Land and buildings £80,000; Fixtures £10,000; Motor vans £16,000; Debtors: ABC Ltd £650, DEF Ltd £325; Cash £600, Bank £3,800; Petty cash £60.	
	Liabilities: Loan £2,000; Creditors: GHI Ltd £1,200, JKL Ltd £625.	
Jan 2	Bought goods on credit from GHI Ltd £1,300. Paid for bus fare £0.95 from petty cash. Paid rent by cheque £220.	
Jan 3	Sold on credit to ABC Ltd £1,000. Paid £2.20 for tea and coffee from petty cash.	
Jan 6	Cash sales lodged £600. Sold on credit to MNO Ltd £800. Bought typing paper from petty cash £3.80.	
Jan 8	Paid advertising by cheque £700. ABC Ltd returned goods £250.	
Jan 9	Sold shop fittings on credit to Moore Ltd £2,000 + VAT @ 21%. Purchased goods by cheque £3,000.	
Jan 11	Purchased goods on credit from PQR Ltd £2,000. Paid taxi fare £4.80 from petty cash.	
Jan 13	Paid GHI Ltd £900 by cheque.	
Jan 16	Returned goods to PQR Ltd £500. Sold goods on credit to DEF Ltd £825. Paid wages by cheque £210.	
Jan 18	Cash sales lodged £120.	
Jan 20	ABC Ltd paid £600 by cheque. Paid £6.50 for postage stamps and £5.60 for typing paper from petty cash.	
Jan 22	Cash purchases £300 paid by cheque.	
Jan 28	Paid bus fare £1.20 from petty cash.	
Jan 30	Paid JKL Ltd £300 by cheque.	
Jan 31	Restored the petty cash Imprest by cheque.	

Q2. Feb 1   Assets: Cash £500; Petty cash £80; Premises £50,000; Motor vans £35,000; Debtors: STS Ltd £600, MNM Ltd £1,600.

Liabilities: Creditors: POP Ltd £1,200, FGF Ltd £380.

Feb 2   Paid for tea and coffee £1.30 and envelopes £2.60 from petty cash. Sold goods on credit to STS Ltd £1,300.

Feb 3   Cash sales £300. Paid wages by cheque £360.

Feb 4   Purchases on credit from POP Ltd £600. Paid £4.20 bus fare and £1.00 for raffle ticket from petty cash.

Feb 5   STS Ltd returned goods £300. Purchased goods by cheque £2,000. Paid advertising £80 cash.

Feb 8   Paid cleaning £8 and £1.80 postage from petty cash. Paid FGF Ltd £350 by cheque.

Feb 10 Sold on credit to QRQ Ltd goods for £1,000. Returned goods to POP Ltd £50.

Feb 15 Cash sales lodged £1,000. MNM Ltd paid £1,200 by cheque.

Feb 18 Paid taxi fare £3.80 and £4.50 for postage stamps from petty cash.

Feb 20 Purchased shop equipment £200 + 21% VAT on credit from Office Exec Ltd.

Feb 23 Purchased goods on credit from FGF Ltd £330.

Feb 26 Sold goods on credit to STS Ltd £600.

Feb 28 Paid cheque to petty cash to restore the Imprest.

Q3. Mar 1   Assets: Land £100,000; Computers £10,000; Stock £5,000; Cash £1,000; Petty cash £75; Debtors: RSR Ltd £340, TUT Ltd £1,000.

Liabilities: Bank overdraft £1,600; Creditors: VOV Ltd £300, GNG Ltd £950.

Mar 3   Sold on credit to RSR Ltd £600. Paid £2.50 for flowers and £6.50 for postage from petty cash.

Mar 3   Purchased on credit from VOV Ltd £1,000. Paid rent £480 cash.

Mar 5   Cash sales lodged £700. Paid GNG Ltd £250 by cheque. Paid £1.80 for milk from petty cash.

Mar 7   Returned goods to VOV Ltd £200. Paid wages £180 cash.

Mar 9   Sold goods on credit to NIN Ltd £300. Purchases of goods made by cheque £1,000.

Mar 11 Sold a 2-year-old computer £1,200 + VAT @ 21% to N. Ryan Ltd on credit. Paid cleaning £5 from petty cash. Purchased on credit from GNG Ltd £900.

Mar 13 RSR Ltd returned goods £210. TUT Ltd paid £250 by cheque.

Mar 15 Paid £3.60 for flowers and £5.60 for note paper from petty cash. Purchased goods on credit from VOV Ltd £360.

Mar 20 Paid £3.60 bus fare and £5 carpet cleaning from petty cash. NIN Ltd returned goods £60.

Mar 25 Purchased on credit from GNG Ltd £350. Cash purchases £100.

Mar 27 TUT Ltd paid £600 by cheque.

Mar 29 Lodged £200 cash to bank.

Mar 31 Paid cheque to petty cash to restore the Imprest.

Q4. Apr 1   Assets: Premises £110,000; Equipment £30,000; Stock £10,000; Petty cash £80; Cash £370; Debtors: BAB Ltd £650, CDC Ltd £1,350.

Liabilities: Bank overdraft £1,375; Loan £850; Creditors: FGF Ltd £850, GHG Ltd £2,350.

Apr 3   Sold on credit to CDC Ltd £390. Paid taxi fare £11 and £12.30 for typing paper from petty cash.

Apr 5   Cash purchases £250. Paid GHG Ltd £1,500 by cheque.

Apr 8   Bought on credit from JIJ Ltd £3,800. Paid rent by cheque £360.

Apr 9   Cash sales lodged £4,800. Withdrew £100 from bank for office cash.

Apr 10 Sold on credit to BAB Ltd £6,500. Returned goods to JIJ Ltd £800. Paid £5.50 for flowers and £6.50 for carpet cleaning from petty cash.

Apr 14 Paid office expenses £65 by cheque. Purchased two new computer printers on credit from Comp Supplies Ltd £630 + VAT @ 21%.

Apr 16 Returned goods to JIJ Ltd £150 + VAT @ 21%.

Apr 18 Purchased goods on credit from GHG Ltd £2,800. Paid advertising by cheque £160.

Apr 20 Paid bus fares £1.90 and £2.50 for picture frame from petty cash. CDC Ltd returned goods £90.

Apr 24 Paid £2.80 for tea and coffee from petty cash. Paid private car insurance £380 by cheque.

Apr 26 Sold on credit to CDC Ltd £4,000. Paid for window cleaning £6 and lock repair £3 from petty cash.

Apr 27 Cash purchases £100. Paid rent £360 by cheque.

Apr 29 CDC Ltd returned goods £1,000.

Apr 30 Paid cheque to petty cash to restore the Imprest.

Q5. May 1   Asset: Premises £120,000; Computers £18,000; Cash £150; Bank £1,250; Petty cash £60; Debtors: HOH Ltd £150, KIK Ltd £650.

Liabilities: Loan £16,000; Creditors: LOL Ltd £450, MIM Ltd £1,650.

May 3   Paid £8 for taxi and £2.50 for envelopes from petty cash. Sold goods on credit to HOH Ltd £1,500.

May 5   Paid insurance £360 by cheque. Purchased goods on credit from MIM Ltd £2,000. Cash sales £3,000 lodged.

May 7   Paid office cleaning £4 and raffle ticket £2 from petty cash. HOH Ltd returned goods £300.

May 9   Bought on credit from LOL Ltd £3,500. Sold computer for £1,500 + VAT @ 21% on credit to DIY Ltd.

May 11   Returned goods to MIM Ltd £400. Paid for present £3 and postage stamps £4.50 from petty cash.

May 12   Paid rent by cheque £120. Paid MIM Ltd £500 by cheque.

May 14   Cash sales lodged £700. Paid school fees for daughter £300 by cheque.

May 15   Paid £2.20 for registered mail and £1.75 for pens from petty cash. Sold on credit to KIK Ltd £2,800.

May 18   Purchased goods on credit from PIP Ltd £600. HOH Ltd returned goods £300.

May 20   KIK Ltd paid £950 by cheque. Withdrew £100 from bank for office cash. Paid £1.50 for envelopes from petty cash.

May 22   Paid advertising £120.

May 24   Paid £500 to MIM Ltd by cheque. Cash purchases £3,000 by cheque. Paid £6.50 for window cleaning and £5 for repairs from petty cash.

May 27   Paid LOL Ltd £225 by cheque.

May 31   Paid cheque to petty cash to restore the Imprest.

Q6. Jun 1   Assets: Land and buildings £95,000; Motor vehicles £6,000; Fixtures and fittings £18,000; Cash £300; Petty cash £80; Debtors: ROR Ltd £450, SUS Ltd £1,350.

Liabilities: Bank overdraft £1,250; Creditors: TOT Ltd £625, WIW Ltd £850.

Jun 3   Sold on credit to SUS Ltd £1,000. Paid WIW Ltd £200 cash. Paid £3.50 for bus fare and £8.80 for paper from petty cash.

Jun 5   Purchased on credit from TOT Ltd £2,300. Paid rent by cheque £300.

Jun 7   SUS Ltd returned goods £550. Paid £8 for present and £5 for cleaning from petty cash.

Jun 8   Cash sales £4,840 (VAT inclusive). Purchased goods on credit from WIW Ltd £4,600.

Jun 10   Paid private grocery bill from the bank £80.

Jun 12   Sold on credit £6,500 to ROR Ltd. Paid wages by cheque £420.

Jun 14   Paid bus fares of £3.20 and milk for 90p from petty cash. Cash purchases £400.

Jun 15   Returned goods to WIW Ltd £600. Cash sales £200.

Jun 18   ROR Ltd returned goods £300. Paid £2 for newspapers from petty cash.

Jun 19   Lodged £3,000 cash to bank. Returned goods to TOT Ltd £150.

Jun 21   Paid wages by cheque £420.

Jun 24   SUS Ltd paid £1,500 by cheque. Paid rent £300 by cheque.

Jun 26   Bought office equipment on credit from Morgan Ltd £2,500 + VAT @ 21%.

Jun 30   Paid cheque to petty cash to restore the Imprest.

Q7. Jul 1   Assets: Premises £95,000; Fixtures and fittings £35,000; Cash £1,550; Petty cash £80; Debtors: Hand Ltd £1,250, Ryan Ltd £260.

Liabilities: Bank overdraft £900; Rent owed £60; Creditors: Morgan Ltd £605, Donnellan Ltd £1,350.

Jul 2   Cash purchases £300. Envelopes £4.40 and stamps £3.60 bought from petty cash.

Jul 4   Credit sales to Hand Ltd £1,400. Paid rent by cheque £310.

Jul 6   Bought goods on credit from Donnellan Ltd £3,600. Cash sales lodged £1,800. Paid bus fares of £3.20 and window cleaning of £1.60 from petty cash.

Jul 7   Sold fixtures on credit to Lynch Ltd £300 + VAT @ 21%. Paid repairs by cheque £150.

Jul 9   Credit sales to Kelly Ltd £3,600. Purchases £1,754.50 VAT inclusive paid by cheque.

Jul 10   Hand Ltd paid £1,600 by cheque. Returned goods to Donnellan Ltd £600. Paid £3 for flowers and £4.50 for note pads from petty cash.

Jul 11   Paid for private house expenses £80 by cheque. Paid wages £220 by cheque. Bought goods on credit from Morgan Ltd £1,800.

Jul 12   Kelly Ltd returned goods £1,000. Paid rent by cheque £310.

Jul 15   Paid cleaning of £8 and bus fares of £1.50 from petty cash.

Jul 16   Sold on credit to Hand Ltd £600. Kelly Ltd paid £2,500 by cheque. Cash sales £300.

Jul 17   Bought new mugs at £4 and paid £3.60 for postage stamps from petty cash. Paid advertising by cheque £60.

Jul 20   Returned goods to Morgan Ltd £100. Paid salary by cheque £400. Paid £4 for writing pads and £1.50 donation to charity from petty cash.

Jul 22   Paid repairs £150 in cash. Lodged £200 cash to bank.

Jul 24   Bought on credit from Donnellan Ltd £1,000.

Jul 26   Paid Morgan Ltd £500 by cheque. Hand Ltd returned goods £120.

Jul 31   Paid cheque to petty cash to restore the Imprest.

Q8. Aug 1   Assets: Buildings £65,000; Motor vans £10,000; Fixtures £6,000; Cash £310; Bank £2,300; Petty cash £50; Debtors: Nolan Ltd £145, King Ltd £1,200.

          Liabilities: Bank overdraft £6,000; Creditors: Murphy Ltd £1,280, O'Leary Ltd £950.

Aug 2   Cash sales £400. Paid £4 for postage and £5.50 for taxi from petty cash.

Aug 3   Bought goods on credit from Murphy Ltd £1,000. Paid advertising by cheque £180.

Aug 5   Paid window cleaning £6 from petty cash. Bought on credit from O'Leary Ltd £1,000.

Aug 7   Cash purchases £500. Paid private car insurance by cheque £460.

Aug 8   Returned goods to O'Leary Ltd £500. Sold on credit to Nolan Ltd £800. Paid rent £90 by cheque.

Aug 12   King Ltd paid £1,000 by cheque. Paid £1.60 to register a letter from petty cash.

Aug 13   Sold goods on credit to Nolan Ltd £600.

Aug 15   Paid advertising £80 in cash. Nolan Ltd returned goods £150.

Aug 17   Nolan Ltd paid £600 by cheque.

Aug 19   Bought on credit from Murphy Ltd £500. Paid £4 for tea and coffee from petty cash.

Aug 20   Withdrew £200 from bank for cash.

Aug 22   Returned goods to Murphy Ltd £180.

Aug 23   Cash purchases £140. Paid £3.60 for postage and £5.00 for envelopes from petty cash.

Aug 25   Paid advertising £110 by cheque. Paid bus fare of £1.60 from petty cash.

Aug 28   Sold goods on credit to Agnew Ltd £410.

Aug 29   Paid Murphy Ltd £400 by cheque. Note paper £6 and raffle ticket £2 bought from petty cash. Bought new delivery van on credit from Motor Suppliers Ltd £15,000 + VAT @ 21%.

Aug 31   Paid cheque to petty cash to restore the Imprest.

Chapter 11

Bank Reconciliation Statements

Anybody who has a current account receives a bank statement at regular intervals. This is usually monthly for a business, as they would have a lot of transactions. A bank statement shows all transactions that have occurred since the last statement, i.e. opening balance, lodgements, withdrawals and the last figure being the amount in the account at the end of the month.

When the business receives the statement, they check it against their own records, i.e. the bank column in the cash book. The closing balance brought down in the bank column of the cash book should be the same as the final balance figure on the bank statement. If they are not the same, we have to find out why. It is for this reason that we prepare a bank reconciliation statement. We want to account for the differences in the two figures. These differences can occur for several reasons.

1. Items on the bank statement that were not known about when the cash book was being prepared, e.g. standing orders, credit transfers.

2. Items in the cash book that were not on the bank statement. These are lodgements not credited by the bank and cheques written but not yet presented to the bank for payment. These are what are known as timing differences. They will go through to the bank in a few days, but they simply have not yet done so by the end of the month.

3. Errors made in the original cash book.

4. Errors made by the bank on the statement.

'Lodgements not credited' refers to lodgements made that have not yet gone onto the bank account. 'Credited' refers to the fact that the bank shows money lodged as a credit item on the statement, i.e. the bank has a liability, and they owe that money back to the account holder. 'Cheques not presented' refers to payments made where the payee has not yet cashed the cheque.

Procedures for Reconciliation

To reconcile the balances you must prepare

1. An updated bank account, i.e. cash book bank column.

2. A bank reconciliation statement.

An **updated bank account** is where you record items from the bank statement that you did not know about and correct any errors made in the original cash book. It is an extension of the original cash book so it begins with the closing balance brought down.

The following are terms used to describe some transactions that may be recorded on the bank statement.

Standing Order (S.O.) is when the customer has the bank pay a bill automatically from their bank account. The amount is the same each time the payment is made, e.g. loan repayment monthly.

Direct Debit (D.D.) is when the bank pays a bill for the customer at regular intervals. The amount may vary each time, e.g. paying the ESB bill from your account.

Credit Transfer (C/T) is when money is lodged to an account. Anybody can lodge money so long as they know the account number, the bank and branch.

Stamp Duty: This is the tax paid to the government when you write a cheque. The bank takes this from your account every time you get a new cheque book.

Refer to Drawer (R/D) *Cheque* means that the cheque has not been honoured. It is a bounced cheque. You should refer back to the drawer of the cheque. Insufficient funds is the usual reason for a bounced cheque. An incorrectly completed cheque would be another reason for a return.

Debit		**Updated Bank a/c**		**Credit**
	(£)			(£)
The closing balance in the original cash book → Bal b/d		Bank charges		
Credit transfer		S.O.		
		D.D.		
		R/D cheque		
		Bal c/d		
	£			£
This figure is found on the statement, credit column. / Bal b/d*			These are found on the statement debit column.	

* This is now the correct balance for bank.

Note: Any errors made in the cash book are corrected in the updated bank account also. The 'updated bank account' can also be refered to as an 'adjusted cash book (bank column)'.

The bank reconciliation statement is then prepared

Bank Reconciliation Statement

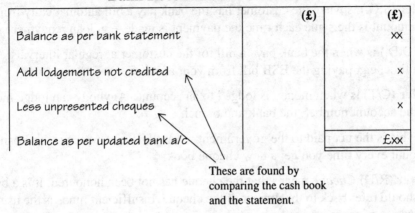

	(£)	(£)
Balance as per bank statement		xx
Add lodgements not credited		x
Less unpresented cheques		x
Balance as per updated bank a/c		£xx

These are found by comparing the cash book and the statement.

Note: Any errors made by the bank are shown here. The error may be added or subtracted.

Example

K. Ryan Ltd received the following bank statement from her bank on June 30.

You are asked to prepare an updated cash book and a reconciliation statement to reconcile the updated bank account with the bank balance below.

Debit   **Cash Book (Bank column)**   **Credit**

Date	Details	(£)	Date	Details	Ch. no.	(£)
Jun 1	Bal b/d	1,980	Jun 5	B. Brady	0156	360
Jun 3	Lodgement	800	Jun 8	Telecom	0157	195
Jun 4	Sales lodged	<2,600	Jun 12	C. Cooke	0158	1,680
			Jun 20	Wages	0159*	860
			Jun 28	D. Daly	0160*	95
			Jun 30	Bal c/d		2,190
		£5,380				£5,380
Jun 30	Bal b/d	2,190				

Note: The entries marked with an * belong on the credit side of the updated cash book, and the entries marked with a < belong on the debit side.

Bank Statement on June 30

		Debit (£)	Credit (£)	Balance (£)
June 1	Balance			1,980.00
Jun 5	C/T		<80.00	2,060.00
Jun 6	Lodgement		800.00	2,860.00
Jun 7	0156	360.00		2,500.00
Jun 10	Stamp duty	1.75*		2,498.25
Jun 14	0158	1,680.00		818.25
Jun 16	S.O.	300.00*		518.25
Jun 18	0157	195.00		323.25
Jun 20	Bank charges	21.60*		301.65
Jun 26	Dividends		<180.00	481.65
Jun 28	Lodgement		95.00	576.65

Note: The entry on June 28th is a lodgement that was made to R. Ryan's account.

Solution

First check that the opening balances are the same. We have a balance brought down of £1,980 in the example above. If the opening bank balance in the cash book is not the same as the opening balance on the statement, then there are unreconciled items from the last month. These can be found on the bank statement and are ignored in this month's updated cash book and reconciliation statement.

Updated Cash Book (Bank column)

Debit Details	(£)	Credit Details	(£)
Bal b/d	2,190.00	Stamp duty	1.75
Credit transfer	80.00	S.O.	300.00
Dividends	180.00	Bank charges	21.60
		Bal c/d	2,126.65
	£2,450.00		£2,450.00
Bal b/d	2,126.65		

This is the correct bank balance figure.

We need to find the items on the bank statement that are not in the cash book.

The debit side in the cash book compares to the credit column on the statement.

The credit side in the cash book compares to the debit column on the statement.

Mark the items on the statement that are not in the original cash book.

Note: The entry dated June 28 on the statement is a bank error and is shown on the reconciliation statement.

Next we need to find the items in the cash book that are not on the statement. Mark each of these.

The entries marked with * are cheques not presented, and the entries marked with < are lodgements not credited.

The Bank Reconciliation Statement

	(£)	(£)
Balance as per bank statement		576.65
Add lodgements not credited		
Sales		2,600.00
		3,176.65
Less unpresented cheques		
0159	860	
0160	95	955.00
		2,221.65
Less bank error		95.00
Balance as per updated bank a/c		£2,126.65

We need to take this out as it is not taken out in the cash book.

Short Questions

1. What is a bank statement? _____

_____

2. Explain a bank overdraft. _____

_____

3. Explain S.O. _____

_____

4. Explain D.D. _____

_____

5. What is a credit transfer?_____

_____

6. Why do lodgements appear in the credit column of a bank statement? _____

_____

7. Who is the payee of a cheque? _____

_____

8. Complete the following bank statement.

		Debit (£)	Credit (£)	Balance (£)
May 1	Balance			65.95
May 5	Lodgement		6,105.00	
May 10	S.O.	150.60		
May 20	Ch. no. 00156	360.90		

9. From what source document is the credit side of the cash book (bank column) written up?

_____

10. What does R/D on a cheque mean? _____

11. List as many possible entries as you can on the Debit and Credit sides below.

Debit   Updated Cash Book (Bank column)   Credit

	(£)		(£)
Bal c/d			

Questions

Q1. From the following, prepare an updated bank account and a bank reconciliation statement for A. Owens on the Sept 30.

Dr   Cash Book (Bank column)   Cr

Date	Details	(£)	Date	Details	Ch. no.	(£)
Sept 1	Bal b/d	526	Sept 5	Rent	0118	360
Sept 3	Cash sales lodged	3,600	Sept 9	P. Smith	0119	1,650
Sept 18	Lodgement	1,600	Sept 20	Wages	0120	320
			Sept 24	S. Price	0121	380
			Sept 30	Bal c/d		3,016
		£5,726				£5,726
Sept 30	Bal b/d	3,016				

Bank Statement on Sept 30

		Debit (£)	Credit (£)	Balance (£)
Sept 1	Balance			526.00
Sept 2	S.O.	120.00		406.00
Sept 5	Lodgement		3,600.00	4,006.00
Sept 10	Bank charges	18.50		3,987.50
Sept 11	0188	360.00		3,627.50
Sept 15	C/T		160.00	3,787.50
Sept 24	0120	320.00		3,467.50
Sept 30	Lodgement		500.00	3,967.50

Note: The lodgement on Sept 30 was made by A. Owens to his private deposit account.

Q2. From the following prepare an updated bank account and a reconciliation statement for B. Boyle on Nov 30.

Dr   **Cash Book (Bank column)**   **Cr**

Date	Details	(£)	Date	Details	Ch. no.	(£)
Nov 1	Bal b/d	1,650	Nov 2	Wages	03176	430
Nov 10	Sales lodged	3,610	Nov 6	M. Maguire	03177	310
Nov 11	Lodgement	360	Nov 11	N. Nolan	03178	68
			Nov 15	ESB	03179	125
			Nov 26	Telecom	03180	350
			Nov 30	Bal c/d		4,337
		£5,620				£5,620
Nov 30	Bal b/d	4,377				

Bank Statement on Nov 30

		Debit (£)	Credit (£)	Balance (£)
Nov 1	Balance			1,650.00
Nov 4	03176	430.00		1,220.00
Nov 6	Bank charges	18.50		1,201.50
Nov 13	03178	68.00		1,133.50
Nov 13	Lodgement		3,610.00	4,743.50
Nov 20	R/D cheque	120.00		4,623.50
Nov 21	Lodgement		360.00	4,983.50
Nov 24	C/T		150.00	5,133.50
Nov 25	03179	125.00		5,008.50
Nov 29	04416	910.00		4,098.50

Note: The entry on Nov 29 was found to be a cheque written by another customer of the bank.

Q3. From the following prepare, an updated bank account and a reconciliation statement for C. Cryan on the Dec 31.

Dr   **Cash Book (Bank column)**   **Cr**

Date	Details	(£)	Date	Details	Ch. no.	(£)
Dec 6	Lodgement	1,600	Dec 1	Bal b/d		1,540
Dec 14	Lodgement	225	Dec 2	Wages	0156	360
			Dec 5	M. Magee	0157	50
			Dec 9	L. Lee	0158	460
			Dec 14	S. Smyth	0159	35
			Dec 21	T. Tuite	0160	568
			Dec 28	W. Walsh	0161	36
Dec 31	Bal c/d	1,224				
		£3,049				£3,049
			Dec 31	Bal b/d		1,224

Bank Statement on Dec 31

		Debit (£)	Credit (£)	Balance (£)
Dec 1	Balance			1,540.00 dr
Dec 4	0156	360.00		1,900.00 dr
Dec 5	S.O. -- EBS	185.00		2,085.00 dr
Dec 8	Lodgement		1,600.00	485.00 dr
Dec 10	0158	460.00		945.00 dr
Dec 11	R/D cheque	180.00		1,125.00 dr
Dec 15	C/T		360.00	765.00 dr
Dec 22	Bank charges	25.60		790.60 dr
Dec 27	C/T		410.00	380.60 dr
Dec 28	0160	568.00		948.60 dr
Dec 30	Lodgement		610.00	338.60 dr

Note: The lodgement on Dec 30 was made to C. Cryan's private account.

Q4. From the following prepare an updated bank account and a reconciliation statement for S. Sweeney on Oct 31.

Dr   **Cash Book (Bank column)**   **Cr**

Date	Details	(£)	Date	Details	Ch. no.	(£)
Oct 1	Balance	1,200	Oct 5	ESB	02516	260
Oct 4	Lodgement	600	Oct 7	Wages	02517	360
Oct 22	Lodgement	1,800	Oct 15	M. McEvoy	02518	1,600
			Oct 20	R. Rooney	02519	1,890
			Oct 27	P. Power	02520	3,600
Oct 31	Bal c/d	4,110				
		£7,710				£7,710
			Oct 31	Bal b/d		4,110

Bank Statement on Oct 31

		Debit (£)	Credit (£)	Balance (£)
Oct 1	Balance			1,200.00
Oct 5	Lodgement		600.00	1,800.00
Oct 7	Bank charges	14.60		1,785.40
Oct 8	S.O.	120.00		1,665.40
Oct 10	02517	360.00		1,305.40
Oct 12	C/T		300.00	1,605.40
Oct 16	02516	260.00		1,345.40
Oct 17	03317	190.00		1,155.40
Oct 25	02519	1,890.00		734.60 dr
Oct 28	Dividends		425.00	309.60 dr

Note: The cheque on Oct 17 was drawn on R. Sweeney's account and not on S. Sweeney's.

Q5. From the following prepare an updated bank account and a reconciliation statement for T. Traynor on Jan 31.

Dr   **Cash Book (Bank column)**   **Cr**

Date	Details	(£)	Date	Details	Ch. no.	(£)
Jan 1	Balance	750	Jan 3	ESB	0675	210
Jan 10	Sales lodged	3,410	Jan 8	Wages	0676	630
Jan 31	Lodgement	2,160	Jan 10	P. Pratt	0677	1,450
			Jan 15	Y. Yale	0678	310
			Jan 21	M. Moore	0679	36
			Jan 28	N. Nice	0680	1,451
			Jan 30	O. Ollie	0681	380
			Jan 30	Bal c/d		1,853
		£6,320				£6,320
Jan 31	Bal b/d	1,853				

Bank Statement on Jan 31

		Debit (£)	Credit (£)	Balance (£)
Jan 1	Balance			1,050.00
Jan 2	0671	300.00		750.00
Jan 3	C/T		510.00	1,260.00
Jan 5	0675	210.00		1,050.00
Jan 7	S.O.	810.00		240.00
Jan 12	0677	1,450.00		1,210.00 dr
Jan 13	Lodgement		3,410.00	2,200.00
Jan 18	Bank charges	31.00		2,169.00
Jan 23	0679	36.00		2,133.00
Jan 27	0678	310.00		1,823.00
Jan 28	0676	630.00		1,193.00

Q6. From the following prepare an updated bank account and a reconciliation statement for W. Wright on Feb 29.

Dr   **Cash Book (Bank column)**   **Cr**

Date	Details	(£)	Date	Details	Ch. no.	(£)
Feb 1	Balance	1,450	Feb 2	Telecom	01845	195
Feb 7	Lodgement	4,360	Feb 4	M. Monks	01846	2,105
Feb 21	Sales lodged	1,463	Feb 6	O. Butler	01847	195
			Feb 13	ESB	01848	210
			Feb 20	Wages	01849	416
			Feb 21	P. Pryor	01850	1,416
			Feb 27	Q. Quinn	01851	310
			Feb 29	Bal c/d		2,426
		£7,273				£7,273
Feb 29	Bal b/d	2,426				

Bank Statement on Feb 29

		Debit (£)	Credit (£)	Balance (£)
Feb 1	Balance			1,657.00
Feb 1	S.O.	410.00		1,247.00
Feb 4	01845	195.00		1,052.00
Feb 5	01830	207.00		845.00
Feb 10	Lodgement		4,360.00	5,205.00
Feb 11	01847	195.00		5,010.00
Feb 15	C/T		399.00	5,409.00
Feb 16	01848	210.00		5,199.00
Feb 22	01849	416.00		4,783.00
Feb 26	01850	1,416.00		3,367.00
Feb 28	Bank charges	26.75		3,340.25
Feb 29	Stamp duty	1.75		3,338.50
Feb 29	Lodgement		560.00	3,898.50

Note: The lodgement on Feb 29 was made by N. Wright to her private account.

Q7. From the following prepare an updated bank account and a reconciliation statement for N. Walsh on the Mar 31.

Dr   **Cash Book (Bank column)**   **Cr**

Date	Details	(£)	Date	Details	Ch. no.	(£)
Mar 1	Balance	365	Mar 3	Rent	01466	310
Mar 5	Sales lodged	2,610	Mar 5	A. Apple	01467	1,410
Mar 23	Lodgement	3,106	Mar 6	ESB	01468	310
			Mar 7	B. Bradley	01469	1,436
			Mar 15	Wages	01470	960
			Mar 20	C. Cooke	01471	1,610
Mar 31	Bal c/d	288	Mar 27	D. Drake	01472	333
		£6,369				£6,369
			Mar 31	Bal b/d		288

Bank Statement on Mar 31

		Debit (£)	Credit (£)	Balance (£)
Mar 1	Balance			365.00
Mar 2	S.O.	106.00		259.00
Mar 5	01466	310.00		51.00 dr
Mar 8	Lodgement		2,610.00	2,559.00
Mar 9	01468	310.00		2,249.00
Mar 16	01470	960.00		1,289.00
Mar 25	lodgement		3,106.00	4,395.00
Mar 26	C/T		600.00	4,995.00
Mar 27	Bank charges	26.70		4,968.30
Mar 28	01570	205.00		4,763.30
Mar 29	01471	1,610.00		3,153.30
Mar 30	R/D cheque	145.60		3,007.70

Note: Cheque number 01570 was written by A. Walsh.

Chapter 12

Theory

In addition to the bookkeeping records that you need to know, you will also need to be familiar with the terminology that is used. The following exercises will help you review all bookkeeping terminology covered to date.

Exercise 1   Place the following source documents under the appropriate heading, indicating where they are written up: Credit notes sent, Cheque stubs, Invoices received, Receipts issued, Credit notes received, Debit notes received, Invoices sent.

Purchases Day Book	Sales Day Book	Purchase Returns Day Book	Sales Returns Day Book	Cheque Payments Page	Cash Receipts Page

Exercise 2   Explain (i) 'Debtors'

_____

_____

_____

           (ii) 'Creditors' _____

_____

_____

_____

Exercise 3   What is a trade discount?

_____

_____

_____

Exercise 4   Explain 'Discount Allowed'.

_____

_____

_____

Exercise 5   Explain 'Discount Received'.

_____

_____

_____

Exercise 6   Name the three parties to a cheque.

(i) _____

(ii) _____

(iii) _____

Exercise 7   Explain VAT.

_____

_____

_____

Exercise 8   Name three controls (accounts) that can be prepared to check the accuracy of the bookkeeping.

(i) _____

(ii) _____

(iii) _____

Exercise 9   What is a bank overdraft?

_____

_____

_____

Exercise 10   Why are folios used?

_____

_____

_____

Exercise 11   How is an opening bank overdraft shown in the cash book?

_____

Exercise 12 What is an asset? Give two examples.

(i) _____

(ii) _____

Exercise 13 What is a liability? Give 2 examples.

(i) _____

(ii) _____

Exercise 14 What is the capital of a business?

_____

_____

_____

Exercise 15 How is capital calculated?

_____

_____

Exercise 16 Why is capital shown as a credit balance in the general ledger?

_____

_____

_____

Exercise 17 What is a contra entry? Give one example.

_____

_____

_____

Exercise 18 What is the Imprest system?

_____

_____

_____

Exercise 19 Sales on credit to N. Noonan are £10,285 inclusive of VAT @ 21%. Complete the entry for this in the Sales Day Book below.

Date	Details	F	Sales (£)	VAT (£)	Total (£)

Exercise 20   When are invoices received?

_____

Exercise 21   List two reasons for receiving a credit note?

(i) _____

(ii) _____

Exercise 22   What does a credit balance brought down in a creditors account at the end of the month mean?

_____

_____

_____

Exercise 23   List three reasons why a trial balance might not balance.

(i) _____

(ii) _____

(iii)_____

Exercise 24   How might a business check that the creditors accounts have been accurately maintained?

_____

_____

_____

Exercise 25   Explain bank charges.

_____

_____

_____

Exercise 26   What does a referral charge mean if it appears on a bank statement?

_____

_____

_____

Exercise 27   What is an invoice?

_____

_____

_____

Exercise 28 What does 'dr' mean after a balance figure on a bank statement?

_____

_____

_____

Exercise 29 Why might a cash discount be given?

_____

_____

_____

Exercise 30 Convert the following 'T' account to a continuous presentation.

Debtors Ledger

Debit   A. Bunce a/c   **Credit**

Date	Details	F	(£)	Date	Details	F	(£)
Jun 1	Bal b/d		1,250.00	Jun 25	S Ret	srdb	650.00
Jun 20	Sales	sdb	3,650.00	Jun 26	Bank	cb	2,000.00
				Jun 30	Balance c/d		2,250.00
			£4,900.00				£4,900.00
May 30	Bal b/d		2,250.00				

Debtors Ledger
A. Bunce a/c

Date	Details	F	Debit (£)	Credit (£)	Balance (£)
Jun 1	Balance c/d				1,250.00

National Council for Vocational Awards

National Vocational Certificate Level 2

Bookkeeping/Double Entry Bookkeeping — Level 2

Thursday, 19 May 1994 9.30 a.m. – 12.30 p.m.

EXAMINATION PAPERS

Instructions to Candidates

There are three Sections to this Paper:

Section A Books of Prime Entry 70% of marks

Section B Bank Reconciliation Statement 20% of marks

Section C Short Answers (Theory) 10% of marks

All names and addresses mentioned are entirely fictitious.

Section A (70%)

Books of Prime Entry

Instructions to Candidates

1   Write up (and analyse) where appropriate the Books of Prime Entry of M. Hand (Sole Trader)

      i.e. Opening Journal

           Day Books

           Cash Book

           Petty Cash Book

2   Post the Books of Prime Entry to the ledgers.

3   Extract a Trial Balance.

4   Prepare a Debtors Control a/c to check the accuracy of your Accounts.

Notes

(a) Supply your own document numbers where appropriate.

(b) Petty Cash Book is recorded with 5 Analysis columns, Stationery, Cleaning, Postage, Travel and Sundries.

(c) All purchases, sales and returns are VAT exclusive. The VAT rate is 21%.

(d) Cash is held in the office safe and cheques are lodged on day of receipt.

Assets and Liabilities on October 1 are as follows:

Oct 1   Premises £70,000; Office Equipment £18,000; Fixtures and Fittings £14,000; Cash £550; Bank Overdraft £2,310; Petty Cash £100;

Debtors: Moore Ltd £363; Carey Ltd £136;

Creditors: Walsh Ltd £189; Brodin Ltd £487.

The following transactions took place during the month of October:

Oct 1   Sold goods on credit to Carey Ltd £380. Bought note paper from Petty Cash £18, Voucher No. 9.

Oct 3   Purchased goods on credit from Brodin Ltd £560.

Oct 4   Bought milk and sugar from Petty Cash £6.50, Voucher No. 10. Paid Wages by cheque £385. Cash Sales £60 money lodged.

Oct 6   Returned goods to Brodin Ltd £184.

Oct 10   Paid Advertising by cheque £38. Bought cleaning cloths out of Petty Cash £3.60, Voucher No. 11.

Oct 12   Cash Sales £200. Paid Walsh Ltd by cheque £90.

Oct 13   Purchased filing cabinets on credit from Office Supplies Ltd £95.

Oct 16   Sold goods on credit to Moore Ltd £650. Paid for postage out of Petty Cash £11.20, Voucher No. 12.

Oct 17   Paid for Taxi out of Petty Cash £11.40, Voucher No. £13. Carey Ltd paid by cheque £80.

Oct 20   Purchased goods on credit from Walsh Ltd £320. Paid for cleaning materials out of Petty Cash £1.80, Voucher No. 14.

Oct 22   Carey Ltd paid by cheque £90. Paid postage £7.30 out of Petty Cash, Voucher No. 15.

Oct 23   Sold goods on credit to Moore Ltd £650. Paid Brodin Ltd £500 by cheque.

Oct 24   Carey Ltd returned goods £100. Paid Advertising by cheque £18.

Oct 25   Returned goods to Walsh Ltd £80. Paid Wages by cheque £380. Paid bus fare £1.80 from Petty Cash Voucher No. 16.

Oct 26   Paid for taxi £10.20 and milk £6.10 from Petty Cash, Vouchers No. 17 and 18. M. Hand paid for private house insurance £120 by cheque from the business bank a/c.

Oct 27   Bought envelopes from Petty Cash £8.60, Voucher No. 19. Purchased goods £300 by cheque. Lodged all Cash except £60.

Oct 28   Cash Sales £410. Money lodged.

Oct 29   Paid cheque to Petty Cash to restore the Imprest amount.

Section B (20%)

Bank Reconciliation

Instructions to Candidates

Set out below is the Bank a/c and Bank Statement of M. Wyse for the Month of March 1994.

Cash Book (Bank Column)

		£			Ch. No.	£
March 1	Balance c/d	1,056	March 3	C. Byrne	107	361
March 6	Lodgement	631	March 5	Wages	108	160
March 13	Sales (lodged)	1,063	March 8	A. Ayer	109	260
March 25	Sales (lodged)	710	March 9	Advertising	110	460
			March 15	R. Reid	111	350
			March 21	R. Power	112	306
			March 31	Balance	c/d	1,563
		£3,460				£3,460
March 31	Balance b/d	£1.563				

Bank Statement on 31/3/94

		Debit	Credit	Balance
March 1	Balance c/d			1,056
March 3	Bank charges	25		1,031
March 6	No. 107	361		670
March 7	No. 108	160		510
March 7	L. Long, (RD cheque)	90		420
March 8	Lodgement		631	1,051
March 18	No. 110	460		591
March 18	Lodgement		1,063	1,654
March 20	Credit Transfer		300	1,954
March 25	No. 112	306		1,648
March 26	Standing order	155		1,493
March 28	A.T.M.	25		1,468
March 28	No. 363	60		1,408

Note: The £60 (cheque no. 363) entered on the bank statement on March 28 was debited in error to M. Wyse's account.

You are required to:

(a)   Prepare an adjusted Cash book showing M. Wyse's correct balance.

(b)   Reconcile the Adjusted Cash book with the Bank Statement.

Section C (10%)

Short Answer Questions

Explain each of the following terms clearly. Illustrate your answers with examples/applications where appropriate.

(i)   Credit Notes received

(ii)   Creditor

(iii)   Capital

(iv)   Bank Charges

(v)   Contra Entry

National Council for Vocational Awards

Bookkeeping/Double Entry Bookkeeping Level 2

Tuesday 23rd May 1995 2.00 p.m. – 5.00 p.m.

Instructions to Candidates

Write your Examination Number on your Answer Book.

There are three Sections in this Examination.

Section A Books of Prime Entry (70%)

Section B Bank Reconciliation Statement (20%)

Section C Short Answer Questions (Theory) (10%)

Candidates are required to answer **all** sections.

Return the **Answer Book** to the superintendent at the end of the examination.

Section A (70%)

Books of Prime Entry

Instructions to Candidates

1. Write up and analyse where appropriate the Books of Prime Entry of B. Morgan (Sole Trader)

    i.e. Opening Journal

    Day Books

    Cash Book

    Petty Cash Book.

2. Post the Books of Prime Entry to the ledgers.

3. Extract a Trial Balance.

Notes

(a) Marks will be awarded for neatness and proper use of folios.

(b) Supply your own document numbers where appropriate.

(c) Petty Cash Book is recorded with 5 Analysis columns, Stationery, Cleaning, Postage, Travel and Sundries.

(d) All purchases, sales and returns are VAT exclusive. The VAT rate is 21%.

(e) Cash is held in the office, and cheques are lodged on day of receipt.

Assets and Liabilities on April 1 are as follows:

Apr 1   Land and Buildings £100,000, Motor Vans £35,000, Equipment £16,000, Cash £430, Bank £1,500, Petty Cash £80.

Debtors: C. Ryan £1,800, G. O'Reilly Ltd. £900.

Creditors: K. McGuirk Ltd £690, A. Monks Ltd. £1,450.

The following transactions took place during the month of April:

Apr 1   Sold goods on credit to C. Ryan £1,400. Paid rent by cheque £3,600. Paid cleaning £20.50 from Petty Cash, Voucher No. 31.

Apr 4   Paid oil bill by cheque £290. Bought postage stamps £8.60 from Petty Cash, Voucher No. 32.

Apr 5   Bought goods on credit from A. Monks Ltd. £1,680. G. O'Reilly Ltd. returned goods £420.

Apr 8   Cash sales £8,000. Sold equipment on credit to Breen Ltd. £320. Paid for taxi £10 from Petty Cash, Voucher No. 33.

Apr 11 Purchases £6,000 by cheque.

Apr 12 Bought envelopes from Petty Cash £8.20, Voucher No. 34. Purchased goods on credit from K. McGuirk Ltd. £3,260.

Apr 13 Paid repairs £590 by cheque. Paid K. McGuirk Ltd. £600 by cheque. Sold goods on credit to G. O'Reilly Ltd. £1,350.

Apr 14 Bought newspapers from Petty Cash £1.80, Voucher No. 35.

Apr 16 Paid Wages by cheque £860.

Apr 19 Purchased goods by cheque £4,400. C. Ryan paid £1,300 by cheque.

Apr 21 B. Morgan returned goods to A. Monks Ltd. £250. Paid for parcel post £6.80 from Petty Cash, Voucher No. 36.

Apr 23 C. Ryan returned goods £380. Paid for tea and coffee £6.30 from Petty Cash, Voucher no. 37.

Apr 25 Purchased goods on credit from A. Monks Ltd. £3,680. Lodged £8,600 cash to bank.

Apr 26 Paid £1.35 for bus fare from Petty Cash, Voucher No. 38. Paid for private car insurance £610 from business cash.

Apr 27 Sold goods for cash £900, money lodged. Bought flowers for reception £4 from Petty Cash, Voucher No. 39.

Apr 28 Bought Receipt Books £3.20 from Petty Cash, Voucher No. 40. Paid for heating oil £195 by cheque.

Apr 29 G. O'Reilly Ltd, paid £1,800 by cheque. Paid £2 for raffle ticket from Petty Cash, Voucher No. 41.

Apr 30 Paid cheque to Petty Cash to restore the Imprest amount.

Section B (20%)

Bank Reconciliation

The following is the Cash Book (Bank column only) and the Bank Statement of M. Reynolds Ltd. for the month of January 1995.

Cash Book (Bank Column)

		£			Ch. No.	£
Jan 1	Balance c/d	850	Jan 4	C. Clarke	0061	435
Jan 7	Sales lodged	880	Jan 7	E.S.B.	0062	108
Jan 15	Lodgement	1,000	Jan 9	B. Byrne	0063	506
Jan 25	Sales lodged	1,060	Jan 11	C. McNamee	0064	306
			Jan 14	Wages	0065	510
			Jan 21	R. Rooney	0066	620
			Jan 31	Balance c/d		1,305
		£3,790				£3,790
Jan 31	Balance b/d	1,305				

Bank Statement on 31/01/95

		Debit	Credit	Balance
Jan 1	Balance b/d			850.00
Jan 5	Credit Transfer		95.00	945.00
Jan 7	No. 0061	435.00		510.00
Jan 9	No. 0062	108.00		402.00
Jan 9	Lodgement		880.00	1,282.00
Jan 11	Government Stamp Duty	1.75		1,280.75
Jan 16	No. 0065	510.00		770.25
Jan 18	S.O.	280.00		490.25
Jan 18	Lodgement		1,000.00	1,490.25
Jan 22	No. 0064	306.00		1,184.25
Jan 27	Bank charges	24.60		1,159.65
Jan 28	Dividends		250.00	1,409.65
Jan 29	Lodgement		180.00	1,589.65

Note: The entry on January 29 is an amount that M. Reynolds lodged to her private deposit account.

You are required to:

(a) Prepare an Adjusted Cash Book showing M. Reynold's correct balance.

(b) Reconcile the Adjusted Cash Book with the Bank Statement.

Section C (10%)

Short Answer Questions

Explain each of the following terms clearly. Illustrate your answers with examples/applications where appropriate.

(a)   Invoices sent

(b)   Debtors Control

(c)   Bank Overdraft

(d)   V.A.T.

(e)   R/D cheque